Baby's Best Chance

Parents' Handbook of Pregnancy and Baby Care

sixth edition 2005

Library and Archives Canada Cataloguing in Publication Data

Main entry under title:

Baby's best chance : parents' handbook of pregnancy and baby care.

"Sixth edition"
Rev. ed. Previously published in 1998 by MacMillan Canada.
Includes index.
ISBN 0-7726-5371-2

1. Pregnancy – Popular works. 2. Prenatal care –
Popular works. 3. Childbirth – Popular works. 4. Infants –
Care – Popular works. I. British Columbia. Ministry of
Health.

RG525B33 2005   618.2'4   C2005-960123-X

You may purchase this book through Government Publications Services at 1-800-663-6105 or online at www.publications.gov.bc.ca. Special discounts for bulk purchases are available.

Published by Open School BC, Victoria, British Columbia, Canada.

Printed by The Queen's Printer of British Columbia, Canada.

Contents

Preface

Welcome to the sixth edition of *Baby's Best Chance: Parents' Handbook of Pregnancy and Baby Care* published by the Government of British Columbia. The first edition was published in 1979 in honour of the "Year of the Child." This edition has been revised to give parents easy to read information, based on best practices and evidence, to ensure a healthy pregnancy and baby.

Baby-Friendly Initiative

The sixth edition of *Baby's Best Chance* has been revised to meet the Baby-Friendly Initiative criteria. The Baby-Friendly Initiative (BFI) is a global program of the World Health Organization (WHO) and UNICEF to increase hospital and community support for promoting, supporting, and protecting breastfeeding. Accepted criteria have been established for designation of Baby-Friendly hospitals, maternity facilities, and communities.

More information on the Baby-Friendly Initiative can be found at:
www.unicef.org/programme/breastfeeding/baby.htm

Acknowledgements

Many professionals in the province of British Columbia reviewed the information in this handbook. Thanks are given to them all, with a special word of gratitude to Barbara Selwood. Thanks are also given to the people who worked on the previous editions. Their work has made this edition possible.

The Design Team included:

Del Nyberg	Ministry of Health Consultant
Michelle Nicholson	Project Manager
Dini Steyn	Project Coordinator
Carol Orom	Instructional Designer
Cindy Lundy	Consultant
Barbara Selwood	Main Content Reviewer
Janet Bartz	Art Director and Book Designer
Pat McCallum	Illustrator and Cover Designer
Lee McKenzie McAnally	Copy Editor
Ian de Hoog	Cover Photographer
Jaya and Raj Saroya	Photography Models
Carrie Ferguson	Illustration Model
David Lloyd	Illustration Model

Work on this project was guided by a Provincial Advisory Committee comprising:

Anne Caulfield	Past Chair, Public Health Audiology Council
Pat Chisholm	President, BC Association of Pregnancy Outreach Programs
Corinne Eisler	Community Nutritionist, Pacific Spirit Community Health Centre, Vancouver
Barbara Findlay	Registered Nurse, BC NurseLine
Dr. Pam Glassby	Dentist, BC Dental Association
Marit Main	Regional Nursing Practice Advisor, Okanagan, Registered Nurses Association of BC
Becky Milne	Telehealth Nurse, BC NurseLine
Jill Mitchell	Audiologist, Public Health Audiology Council
Candace Porter	Consultant, Early Childhood Development, Ministry of Children and Family Development
Dr. Jill Peacock	Board Member, BC College of Family Physicians
Rose Perrin	Public Health Nursing Leaders Council of BC
Barbara Selwood	Community Perinatal Nurse Consultant, BC Reproductive Care Program, Provincial Public Health Nursing Perinatal Committee
Thais Turner	Speech and Language Pathologist Representative, BC Speech Language Pathology Council for Early Childhood Development
Jennie Walker	Health Director, Three Corners Health Services Society, Williams Lake
Tana Wyman	BC Dental Public Health Committee

Subject Matter Experts who conducted extensive review of the content include:

Eileen Bennewith	Community Nutritionist, Vancouver Island Health Authority
Vera Berard	Registered Midwife, Midwifery Care North Shore, North Vancouver
Marina Green	Clinical Educator/International Board Certified Lactation Consultant, BC Baby-Friendly Network
Lyn Jones	Clinical Resource Nurse, Richmond Hospital, Vancouver Coastal Health
Jennesse Oakhurst	Registered Midwife and International Board Certified Lactation Consultant, Ridge Meadows Midwifery Practice, Maple Ridge

Rose Perrin	Public Health Nursing Leaders Council of BC, Northern Health Authority
Barbara Selwood	Community Perinatal Nurse Consultant, BC Reproductive Care Program
Susan Walter	Clinician/Educator, Vancouver Coastal Health North Shore Community and Family Health

Other professionals who provided specific content review include:

Marilyn Barr	National Center on Shaken Baby Syndrome (USA)
Ron Barr	Centre for Community Child Health Research at the BC Research Institute for Children's and Women's Health
Radhika Bhagat	Provincial Public Health Nurses Early Childhood Development Committee
Doris Bodnar	Reproductive Mental Health, BC Women's Hospital and Health Centre
Susannah Britnell	BC Women's Physiotherapy Department, BC Women's Hospital and Health Centre
Elaine Chong	BC NurseLine (Pharmacy)
Paul Coleman	Income Taxation Branch
Dr. Ray Copes	Director, Environmental Health, BC Centre for Disease Control
Larry Copeland	Director, Food Protection Services, BC Centre For Disease Control
Jan Christilaw	Specialized Women's Health, BC Women's Hospital and Health Centre
Marty Deshaw	Surrey Taxation Canada, Benefit Programs, Canadian Revenue Agency
Azmina Dharamsi	Children's and Women's Health Centre of British Columbia
Mary Falconer	Legal Services Branch, Ministry of Attorney General
Dr. Duncan Farquharson	Obstetrical Medical Consultant, BC Reproductive Care Program
Shanti Gidwani	Options for Sexual Health
Anthea Kennelly	Vancouver Island Health Authority, North Island
Dr. Christine Loock	Sunny Hill Health Centre, BC's Children's Hospital
Dr. Brian Lupton	Pediatric Medical Consultant, BC Reproductive Care Program
Karen Pielak	Epidemiology Services, BC Centre for Disease Control
Nancy Poole	BC Women's Hospital and BC Centre of Excellence for Women's Health

Linda Reid	Child Passenger Safety Network
Dr. Mary Lou Riederer	BC Association of Optometrists
Sonny Senghera	Vehicle Safety Strategies, Insurance Corporation of BC
Dr. Jeffrey Simons	Pediatrician, Prince Rupert
Dr. Paul Thiessen	Pediatrician, Children's and Women's Health Centre of British Columbia
Lois Toms	Ministry of Attorney General
Finola Turgeon	Benefit Programs, Canadian Revenue Agency
Laurie Usher	Audiology Clinical Coordinator, Children's and Women's Health Centre of British Columbia
Sue Wastie	Vancouver Community, Vancouver Coastal Health
Anne Williams	Safe Start Injury Prevention Program, BC Children's Hospital
June Yee	Clinical Pharmacist, Children's and Women's Health Centre of British Columbia
Lori Zehr	Consultant, Chronic Disease Prevention

Thanks to Ministry of Health personnel who contributed to the project, including:

Frankie Best, Janet Carter, Valery Dubenko, Lisa Forster-Coull, Joan Geber, Pauline James, Anne Kent, Roberta L. Moyer, Dr. Malcolm Williamson, and Laurie Woodland.

We also appreciate the feedback provided by our parent focus groups, comprising:

Healthiest Babies Possible (Surrey/Delta/White Rock) participants and *Baby Talk* (Kelowna) participants organized by Christina Sutter and Pam Benson.

Introduction

You're going to have a baby! Congratulations! *Baby's Best Chance: Parents' Handbook of Pregnancy and Baby Care* will help you during your pregnancy and prepare you for the birth of your baby, and the first six months of your baby's life. You can use this book as your main guide to having a successful, healthy pregnancy and giving your baby a good start in life. The months while your baby is developing as a fetus and the first few months of life are very important for the future health and happiness of your child.

As you read this book you will see it is divided into two sections. The first is to help support you during and after your pregnancy. The second section gives you information on getting the best start with your new baby. Every effort has been made to give you information that you can trust. Using this book will help you make sound decisions about your pregnancy and your baby.

Baby's Best Chance: Parents' Handbook of Pregnancy and Baby Care is the first of two books on pregnancy and early childhood development available from the Government of British Columbia. The second book, *Toddler's First Steps,* covers child development from six months to three years. Pick up your copy of *Toddler's First Steps* when your baby is about four months old. You can get it from your public health office or the BC Ministry of Health website at: www.health.gov.bc.ca/cpa/publications/firststeps.pdf.

Welcome to the rewarding and challenging world of parenthood.
Good luck on your new venture!

How to Use this Handbook

How do you read a book? From cover-to-cover, or do you dip in and out seeking specific information? This book is designed for both types of reading. The following components will help you find the information you need, quickly and efficiently.

Contents
The table of contents will help you find a specific topic. Note that the book is divided into two large sections: *Becoming a Parent* and *Your Baby.* Everything to do with you is in the first section and everything to do with your new baby is in the second section.

Page Arrangement
The layout will help you sort information quickly.

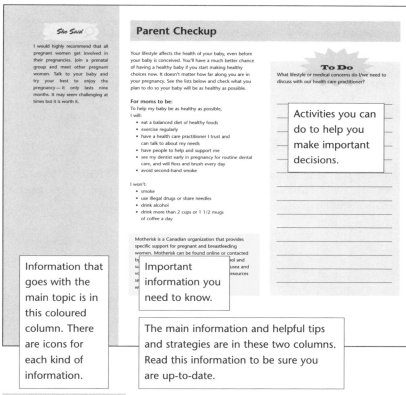

Information that goes with the main topic is in this coloured column. There are icons for each kind of information.

Important information you need to know.

The main information and helpful tips and strategies are in these two columns. Read this information to be sure you are up-to-date.

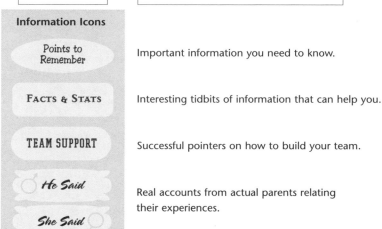

Information Icons	
Points to Remember	Important information you need to know.
FACTS & STATS	Interesting tidbits of information that can help you.
TEAM SUPPORT	Successful pointers on how to build your team.
He Said	Real accounts from actual parents relating their experiences.
She Said	

At the back of the book you'll find:

Resources

Need a phone number or contact information? See the Resources on page 140.

Glossary

Don't know the meaning of some words in this book? Check the Glossary on page 144.

Index

Need to find a topic quickly? See the Index on page 150.

Websites

Throughout this book, there are many references to Internet websites. If you do not have Internet access at home, go to your local public library for free use of a computer with access.

Becoming a Parent

Welcome to parenthood! You will find all kinds of information in this section. Browse through it with your partner to learn about the stages of pregnancy. Find out how to take good care of yourselves, how to handle any discomforts you may be feeling, and the details of birth. There is also a special section on nutrition written especially for pregnant women.

Your Support Team

TEAM SUPPORT

You, the father of your child or your partner, and your baby will benefit from having a team of supportive people. Who can be on your support team? Anyone you trust. For many women, the primary support person is their partner. However, mothers and fathers need more than one support person. They need a health care support team and a personal support team. Remember, support teams vary and are unique to each expectant family.

Who might be on your health care support team?
You might choose among any of these professionals:
- family doctor and/or obstetrician
- registered midwife
- hospital nurses
- public health nurses
- the BC NurseLine
- dentist
- dental hygienist
- prenatal educator
- registered dietitian
- pharmacist
- lactation consultant
- naturopathic physician

To Do
Who will be on your personal support team? Once you have decided, share your plans with them and ask for their commitment. Go to My Team Contact Information on the inside front cover and record their contact information. You will think about your medical support team when reading Choosing Health Care Practitioners.

Who might be on your personal support team?
- your partner, friends
- a social worker
- a doula (trained, supportive labour companion)
- family members
- neighbours
- expectant families from prenatal classes
- community groups
- co-workers
- members of your cultural or religious groups

How can your support team help?
- provide medical expertise
- help you make decisions
- provide emotional support
- provide practical support
- help while you are pregnant
- help at the birth
- help after the birth

A Special Word to Partners
You can be supportive by:
- sharing a healthy lifestyle before, during, and after pregnancy
- sharing in physical exercise
- helping with relaxation techniques
- listening
- attending appointments and prenatal classes
- preparing the home for the new baby
- being involved in the labour and birth
- talking about and planning for parenting
- being actively involved in caring for the baby
- encouraging and helping with breastfeeding
- arranging holidays or leave from work to help with the new baby

Choosing Health Care Practitioners

Throughout this book you will see the term *health care practitioners*. It means doctors, nurses, midwives, or any other medical professionals.

How can you find health care practitioners?

- Ask another health care practitioner, such as a public health nurse or a childbirth educator, for recommendations.

- Call the College of Physicians and Surgeons, College of Family Physicians, or College of Midwives.

- Ask friends for recommendations.

- Call your hospital for a list of doctors accepting new patients.

You should visit your health care practitioner before you decide to become pregnant. However, if you are already pregnant, it is important to have early and regular visits with your health care practitioners. You can also read about pregnancy care and making a healthy baby at BC HealthGuide OnLine: www.bchealthguide.org. Use "pregnancy" as your search term.

To Do

Some questions to ask when choosing your health care practitioners:

- Do they work with families who are pregnant?

- What are their policies regarding phone calls, home visits, on-call coverage?

- What is the length and frequency of office visits?

- Will they be available when you are ready to give birth?

- What are your choices for place of birth? If you plan a home birth, you must consult with a midwife. Doctors in BC do not attend home births.

- Are they open to working with you regarding your birth preferences, such as support people, birth positions, and pain control choices?

- Do they have any routine procedures?

- Will they support you in breastfeeding?

List any other questions you may want to discuss.

_____

_____

_____

Determine who will be on your health care support team. Then go to My Team Contact Information (on the inside front cover) and record the contact information for each of the team members.

FACTS & STATS

In January 1998, midwifery became a formal part of British Columbia's health care system. In this book the term midwife refers to Registered Midwives, as recognized by the College of Midwives of British Columbia.

The Medical Services Plan in British Columbia covers the costs for doctors and midwives, but it will not pay for both a doctor and a midwife during your pregnancy. You will need to select one or the other. Midwives can provide care for normal, low-risk pregnancies in hospital or at home.

I would highly recommend that all pregnant women get involved in their pregnancies. Join a prenatal group and meet other pregnant women. Talk to your baby and try your best to enjoy the pregnancy — it only lasts nine months. It may seem challenging at times but it is worth it.

Also make a journal, something you can show your child later in life so they can see how you felt about them, day by day, while you were expecting. I put in weekly pregnancy photos, ultrasound photos, my thoughts, and details of doctor appointments. Once she is born I will add other details of her life and of course a lot more photos. I think it will be something she will always appreciate.

Parent Checkup

Your lifestyle affects the health of your baby, even before your baby is conceived. You'll have a much better chance of having a healthy baby if you start making healthy choices now. It doesn't matter how far along you are in your pregnancy. See the lists below and check what you plan to do so your baby will be as healthy as possible.

For moms to be:
To help my baby be as healthy as possible,
I will:
- eat a balanced diet of healthy foods
- exercise regularly
- have a health care practitioner I trust and can talk to about my needs
- have people to help and support me
- see my dentist early in pregnancy for routine dental care, and will floss and brush every day
- avoid second-hand smoke

I won't:
- smoke
- use illegal drugs or share needles
- drink alcohol
- drink more than 2 cups or 1 1/2 mugs of coffee a day

For dads to be:
To help my baby be as healthy as possible,
I will:
- eat healthy nutritious foods
- exercise with my partner
- be supportive to my partner
- avoid second-hand smoke

I won't:
- smoke
- use illegal drugs or share needles

To Do
What lifestyle or medical concerns do I/we need to discuss with our health care practitioner?

_____

_____

_____

_____

_____

_____

_____

_____

_____

_____

_____

_____

_____

Lifestyle and Risk Factors

FACTS & STATS

More people die from smoking than from vehicle crashes, alcohol, drugs, suicide, AIDS, and homicide combined. In BC, that's about 5,600 people each year.

Saunas, Hot Tubs, and Hot Baths

Hot tubs and saunas can be relaxing and soothing, but it is important not to increase your inner body temperature. This overheating can increase your developing baby's body temperature. It is important for your baby not to become overheated. Being overheated can affect your baby's healthy development.

If you choose to use a hot tub or sauna:
- Lower the temperature to below 38.9°C.

- Limit your time in the hot tub or sauna to 10 minutes, or less if you feel uncomfortable.

- Have another adult with you.

- Get out right away if you feel dizzy, faint, have rapid pulse, irregular heartbeat, stomach pain, or tingling in feet and hands.

For more information, see the BC HealthFile #27a, *Hot Tubs — Health and Safety Tips,* available at BC HealthGuide at www.bchealthguide.org. You can also get this file at your local public health office.

Getting X-rays and Other Tests

Some medical tests may not be safe for pregnant and breastfeeding women. Before having X-rays, dental X-rays, CT scans, and other tests, be sure to tell the technician you are pregnant or breastfeeding. If you want to learn more about conditions and tests before you take them, see BC HealthGuide OnLine at www.bchealthguide.org.

Taking Medications

If you are pregnant, breastfeeding, or even thinking about having a baby, you may be worried about using medication. Some medicines are safe for use during pregnancy or when breastfeeding; however, others may not be safe.

Safety issues can arise with all types of medication, including:
- those available only by prescription
- those available as over-the-counter or non-prescription products
- natural health products

Check with your doctor, pharmacist, or health care professional for advice on your medication. They can help make sure all your medications are safe to take. Some medications, such as those for mood or seizure disorders, should not be stopped suddenly. If you are unsure, and it is after office hours, you can call the BC NurseLine at 1-866-215-4700 and speak with a pharmacist between the hours of 5 p.m. and 9 a.m. daily.

Smoking

It is best to stop smoking before you plan to become pregnant. Smoking and second-hand smoke are harmful during pregnancy, and after your baby is born. Cigarettes contain many chemicals that cross the placenta into the baby's blood.

If you are pregnant and smoke, now is the time for both you and your partner to stop or reduce the amount you smoke.

The best thing you can do is **quit**.

No one should smoke in your home. A smoke-free home is important for your baby's health and for everyone else in your family.

Partners can help by not drinking. They can also help by being involved with the mother in social activities that don't involve alcohol. Bring a bottle of sparkling apple juice to a friend's house for dinner, or go to a movie instead of a bar or nightclub. A milkshake or juice is a healthy substitute for beer.

To help you quit smoking or reduce the amount you smoke:

- See your health care practitioner.

- Join a stop-smoking program and stick with it.

- Contact Quitnow by phone at 1-877-455-2233 for free, confidential, no-pressure counselling and support from trained specialists. Or you can log onto www.quitnow.ca for support in the privacy of your home.

- Call your public health office, the BC NurseLine at 1-866-215-4700, or check the BC HealthGuide OnLine at www.bchealthguide.org, for information on local stop smoking programs.

- Read the BC HealthFile #30, *Second-Hand Smoke: More Dangerous than You Realize* at www.bchealthguide.org if you need more reasons to quit.

- Ask for the support of your partner, friends, family, and co-workers.

- Buy yourself something special with the money you save.

- If you find that you smoke to deal with stress, find other healthy ways to relax.

- Focus on the health of your baby as a motivator.

Harmful effects of smoking on the mother and father:

- promotes high cholesterol
- increases the risk of cancer of the cervix, infertility, and menstrual problems
- is a powerful stimulant
- is extremely addictive
- causes gum disease
- causes heart and circulatory disease, lung and other cancers, emphysema, and chronic bronchitis

Smoking and exposure to second-hand smoke during pregnancy contribute to a higher risk of:

- slowing your baby's growth and development
- miscarriage
- stillbirth (two to three times higher)
- preterm birth and low birth weight

Smoking and second-hand smoke after birth contribute to a higher risk of:

- Sudden Infant Death Syndrome (SIDS).

- More hospital admissions in the first year of life than children of non-smoking parents. Children of smokers have more ear infections. They also have more illnesses, such as asthma and bronchitis.

- A reduced milk supply in the mother.

- Your baby having colic or inconsolable crying spells. Smoking during pregnancy is associated with an increased risk for colic, but many infants with colic also come from non-smoking households.

- Your child also becoming a smoker.

Drinking Alcohol

How does alcohol affect the fetus?

Drinking alcohol during pregnancy can result in lifelong disabilities for your child. This is called Fetal Alcohol Spectrum Disorder (FASD). Children with FASD have problems with speech and vision, learning problems, poor memory, and poor coordination. They also have difficulty handling emotions. These challenges make it difficult for them to handle even simple daily life tasks.

When you drink during pregnancy, alcohol passes from your bloodstream to the baby. This can have an effect on your baby's development. There is no known safe amount of alcohol that you can drink in pregnancy. Daily drinking and binge drinking (three or more drinks at any one time) are the most risky. Since we don't know any safe level of alcohol use in pregnancy, it is recommended that women don't drink at all during pregnancy.

What are solutions?
- Plan to stop drinking before you become pregnant.

- If you are already pregnant, stop drinking as soon as possible. It is never too late to stop.

If you find it hard to stop drinking:
- Talk to your health care practitioner or someone you trust about services and supports to help you.

- Contact a Pregnancy Outreach Program for assistance.

- Ask for help from a support group or alcohol and drug counsellor.

- Contact Motherisk. See Resources at the back of the book for phone numbers.

- If you cannot stop drinking completely, it is important to reduce the amount you drink. Less is better, none is best.

Using Street Drugs

Illegal drugs and street drugs can be harmful for you and for your developing baby during pregnancy. Like alcohol, these drugs pass through the placenta to the baby.

If you use street drugs during pregnancy, you increase the risk of miscarriage, stillbirth, and preterm delivery. You may also eat poorly, not get enough sleep, and be at risk for diseases such as hepatitis and HIV. Mothers who continue to use street drugs are usually advised not to breastfeed.

Marijuana
Use of marijuana can affect your energy, judgment, and motivation at this important time. Using marijuana during pregnancy can increase your risk of giving birth to your baby prematurely, and it can affect your baby's growth and long-term health.

Cocaine and Methamphetamine (Crystal Meth)
Using stimulants, such as cocaine and crystal meth, can be very harmful to your overall health, affecting your heart rate, energy, sleeping patterns, memory, and mental health. If used during pregnancy, stimulants can cause the premature separation of the placenta from the wall of the uterus. This is a very serious health concern for both you and your baby. Babies are also at risk for Sudden Infant Death Syndrome (SIDS).

Heroin
Using heroin can be risky because of the drug's effects and the use of needles if you inject it. Using heroin in pregnancy can increase the risk of miscarriage and stillbirth. It is important to get help during pregnancy to help you **slowly decrease** your use so your baby does not have withdrawal symptoms, even before it is born. Support for using methadone instead of heroin during pregnancy is available in BC for mothers who cannot stop their heroin use.

Babies born to mothers who have used heroin during pregnancy can have withdrawal symptoms that often start within 72 hours after their birth. At birth, it is important to have medical practitioners help the baby with these symptoms.

After the withdrawal period, children whose mothers used heroin during pregnancy may do well in the long term, if they were not exposed to other risks and if they are raised in a positive environment.

Inhalants
Solvents (such as glue, gasoline, paint thinner and cleaning fluids) and aerosols (such as compressed gases from hairspray and spray paint cans) can be very risky for your health when breathed in. In pregnancy they can affect your blood pressure and increase the risk of miscarriage. Babies of mothers who use solvents in pregnancy are at risk for a range of physical birth defects. There is also concern that babies born to mothers who use inhalants, or come in contact with them a lot in pregnancy, may be at risk for long lasting mental health and behaviour problems similar to Fetal Alcohol Spectrum Disorder.

Points to Remember

Motherisk is a Canadian organization that provides specific support for pregnant and breastfeeding women. Motherisk can be found online or contacted by phone. It has separate help lines for alcohol and substance use. There is also a helpline for nausea and vomiting. For more information, check the Resources section at the back of the book or visit www.Motherisk.org.

Points to Remember

If you find it hard to stop using street drugs, there are specialized services available to help. If you can't stop drug use, there are ways to reduce harm to you and your baby. There are support services in your community including:
- health care providers, such as street nurses and clinics
- pregnancy outreach programs

Services can be found by calling the Alcohol & Drug Information and Referral Service, toll-free at 1-800-663-1441.

Living with Abuse

Intimate partner violence is a pattern of physical, sexual, or emotional violence. It uses power and control. Twenty-five to thirty percent of women have been physically harmed by their partner or boyfriend at sometime in their lives. Most women who are abused do not report it. Forty percent of wife abuse starts in a women's first pregnancy. Only three percent of women who were abused during their pregnancy told their health care practitioners.

If your partner used physical, verbal, emotional, or sexual abuse in the past, this may get worse once you are pregnant and after you have the baby. You are not the only one at risk if your partner abuses you. Your baby is also at risk. Seek help and safety. You can start by talking to your health care practitioner. She or he will put you in touch with the right resources. Do not feel ashamed. It is not your fault.

Sexually Transmitted Infections

- Some sexually transmitted infections (STIs) can be cured and others cannot.

- Some STIs can cause problems with your pregnancy or harm your baby.

You can protect yourself and your baby by using condoms, especially if you are not in a steady relationship. For example, condoms will reduce your risk of catching herpes (an infected partner may have symptoms you cannot see). It is important for both your health and your baby's health that you talk with your health care practitioner if you have, or think you may have, an STI, such as herpes, hepatitis B, or HIV. There are treatments available for you and your baby.

The charts on the next two pages provide information on some STIs that could affect your pregnancy, be a risk to your baby, or increase your risk of preterm labour.

To Do

- Tell my health care practitioner about any history of sexually transmitted infections (STIs).

- Tell my health care practitioner if I suspect I have been exposed to an STI, and get tested.

- Talk with my partner about our sexual history.

- Use a condom for six months with a new sexual partner and be tested for STIs.

- Do not share needles or have multiple sexual partners.

- Read the BC HealthFiles series on Sexually Transmitted Diseases found at: www.bchealthguide.org.

You can reduce the chance of getting STIs, including HIV, by avoiding high-risk activities, such as:
- having multiple partners
- injecting or using street drugs
- sharing needles
- having a number of sexual partners and not using condoms
- engaging in anal sex without condoms

If you suspect that you have been exposed to an STI, talk with your health care practitioner, public health nurse, or call the BC NurseLine at 1-866-215-4700 right away.

Motherisk offers information and counselling to Canadians about HIV and other STIs. Call the toll-free health line at 1-888-246-5840 or visit www.Motherisk.org.

Sexually Transmitted Infections that Cannot be Cured

Infection	Risks/Complications	Method of Transfer	Treatment/Comments
Herpes Diagnosed by culture of lesion or vaginal secretions.	**Mom:** Can have blisters/sores in genital area only once or she may have outbreaks every once in a while. She may not know she is carrying the virus. Avoid intercourse if a lesion is present. Avoid oral sex if your partner has a cold sore. Using condoms during sex helps, but it is not a guarantee that you won't get herpes. **Baby:** Has poor energy, fever, poor weight gain, infection of skin, eyes, mouth. There can be severe brain injury or death.	Can transfer in the birth canal during birth.	**Mom:** No cure. Antiviral drugs are used to treat outbreaks. If herpes sore is in genital area at time of labour, a caesarean birth is recommended. This is to prevent transfer to the baby. **Baby:** Antiviral drugs can be given if baby develops neonatal herpes.
Hepatitis B Diagnosed by blood test. (Also spread by contact with infected blood.)	**Mom:** Carrier for life; risk for liver disease and liver cancer later in life. **Baby:** Without treatment, will become a carrier for life.	Can transfer during birth.	**Mom:** If exposed during pregnancy, early treatment with Hepatitis B immune globulin (HBIG) and Hep B vaccine can prevent disease. **Baby:** HBIG and Hep B vaccine at birth if mother (or other caretaker) is a carrier and follow-up vaccinations can prevent disease.
Human Immuno-deficiency Virus (HIV) Diagnosed by blood test.	**Mom:** HIV can develop into AIDS. Adults with AIDS have a shortened lifespan.	Can cross placenta during pregnancy and can transfer to baby during birth. Is also possible to transfer through breastfeeding.	**Mom:** No cure; treatment with antiviral drugs during pregnancy and during labour to reduce risk of passing virus to baby. **Baby:** Antiviral medication given for six weeks after birth.

Bacterial Sexually Transmitted Infections that Can be Cured

Infection	Risks/Complications	Method of Transfer	Treatment/Comments
Chlamydia Diagnosed by a culture of vaginal discharge.	**Mom:** May have pain when peeing, vaginal discharge, or no symptoms. Increased risk of preterm labour, premature rupture of membranes. **Baby:** Pneumonia, eye infections.	Can transfer in the birth canal during birth.	**Mom:** Antibiotics. **Baby:** Antibiotics; routine eye treatment with antibiotic ointment soon after birth prevents infection in baby's eyes.
Gonorrhea Diagnosed by a culture of vaginal discharge.	**Mom:** May have lower abdominal pain, vaginal discharge, pain when peeing, or no symptoms. **Baby:** Eye infections if mother not treated during pregnancy.	Can transfer through birth canal into uterus and to baby, during pregnancy or during birth.	**Mom:** Antibiotics. **Baby:** Antibiotics placed in the eyes of newborns shortly after birth.
Bacterial Vaginosis Diagnosed by culture of vaginal secretions.	**Mom:** May have vaginal discharge, vaginal itching or burning; sometimes no symptoms. Increased risk of preterm labour, premature rupture of membranes, infection during labour or postpartum. **Baby:** Preterm birth.	Can transfer through birth canal into uterus and to baby.	**Mom:** Antibiotics. **Baby:** Care needed for preterm birth.
Syphilis Diagnosed by a blood test.	**Mom:** May have small, painless sore in genital area within two months of exposure. Illness (about six weeks after sore heals) — fever, rash, headache, swollen glands. If not treated can cause problems years later, e.g. nervous system, eyes, heart. Possible preterm labour. **Baby:** Possible stillbirth; congenital syphilis with physical and mental problems.	Can cross the placenta during pregnancy and can transfer during birth.	**Mom and Baby:** Antibiotics during pregnancy. **Baby:** Antibiotics if mother not treated during pregnancy.

Stages of Pregnancy

Pregnancy affects every system of your body, not just your uterus. The chart, beginning on the next page, lists some of the common changes you may experience in pregnancy. It also suggests what you can do to stay comfortable.

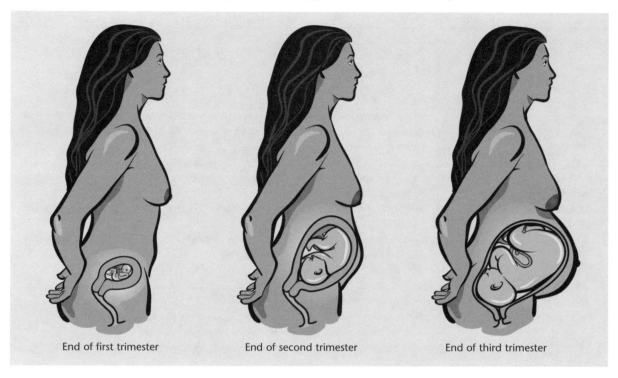

End of first trimester   End of second trimester   End of third trimester

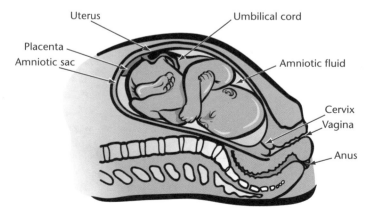

Uterus

Umbilical cord

Placenta

Amniotic sac

Amniotic fluid

Cervix

Vagina

Anus

I thought that being pregnant would be fantastic, since my mother had good pregnancies. I was shocked that instead of having that "glow," I was nauseated and vomiting. Then I ended up in the hospital early, with bleeding, and had a caesarean section birth. But in the end, the pregnancy seemed like such a short time compared to parenting, which lasts forever.

1st
trimester mother

TEAM SUPPORT

- Don't smoke, drink, or use drugs.

- If your partner smokes, encourage her to stop.

- Expect and accept mood changes.

- Share meal preparation, especially if your partner is nauseated.

- Take over some responsibilities if your partner is feeling tired.

- Go to prenatal checkups with your partner.

FACTS & STATS

Nausea and vomiting bother up to 80% of pregnant women to some degree. For many women this can go on beyond 20 weeks.

What's Happening?	Now What?
your periods will stop and you may have tender or painful breasts	• wear a comfortable, supportive bra
unexpected mood changes	• this is normal • focus on yourself and the changes you are going through • talk with the people around you **Check in:** If you are feeling down for longer than seven days and the things that used to give you joy no longer do, you may have depression. See page 86. Talk with your health care practitioner now about how you are feeling.
feeling excitement, fear, or uncertainty about being a parent	• it is normal to have many feelings about a new pregnancy • share your feelings • spend time with other new parents, a pregnancy support group, or new parent group Call your public health office for information on pregnancy/perinatal support groups. You can find the number in the blue pages of your phone book. You can also ask your health care practitioner.
fatigue (feeling tired and sleepy)	• this is normal; rest whenever you can • have periods of activity and then of rest; stop before you become overtired • eat small meals several times a day and drink plenty of water • if you are working, try to rest on your breaks and at lunchtime **Feeling tired — how much is normal?** You may not feel tired at all, or you may be falling asleep during the day. Both are normal.
headaches (due to hormonal and postural changes)	• headaches are quite common • practice good posture • eat small, nutritious meals several times a day • drink plenty of water daily • avoid activities that cause eyestrain • get plenty of sleep at night and rest during the day • have your neck, shoulders, face, and scalp massaged • apply a cool or warm washcloth to your forehead and the back of your neck • drink two cups of water and take some acetaminophen • talk to your health care practitioner if your headache does not go away

What's Happening?	Now What?
need to pee more often	• drink water, milk, and juice instead of coffee, tea, or colas
morning sickness (nausea and vomiting)	• eat smaller amounts of food every one to two hours during the day • try to follow *Canada's Food Guide to Healthy Eating* as much as possible; however, ignoring the guidelines for a short time won't hurt your baby • if your iron or prenatal supplements make you feel queasy, take them with a slushy-type drink • try taking a liquid form of vitamins • try to keep taking your folic acid supplement even if you can't take prenatal vitamins for a period of time • eat whatever appeals to you during this time • avoid fatty and fried foods • drink fluids such as apple juice, ginger ale, water, and clear black tea • don't drink red raspberry leaf herbal tea as it may cause uterine contractions • try eating cold meals to avoid food smells, or have someone else cook • have fresh air in the bedroom while resting, and in the kitchen while cooking • try not to get too tired • wear loose clothing around your chest and waist If you do vomit, rinse your mouth with water. You can also use a fluoride mouth rinse. This will help protect your teeth from the damage of stomach acids.
increased vaginal secretions (thin and milky)	• wear small pads, cotton underwear, and looser slacks • shower or bathe often • contact your health care practitioner if there is itchiness or frothy, smelly, or coloured discharge
bigger or painful breasts and darkening of the areola (brown part around the nipple) with small lumps becoming visible	• wear a supportive bra for comfort, even at night if it helps
light-headedness or feeling faint	• stand up slowly • maintain good posture and exercise regularly • eat regularly and often
shortness of breath	• this is usually normal, but check with your health care practitioner if there is a history of heart problems in your family

Points to Remember

See your health care practitioner if you:

• are sick most of the time and can't keep fluids or food down

• vomit more than 5 times a day

• have lost more than 5% of your pre-pregnant weight

• pee less than 3 times in 24 hours

If you can't manage your nausea and vomiting, talk with your health care practitioner about medication you can take to help.

You can also contact Motherisk Nausea and Vomiting of Pregnancy Helpline, toll-free at 1-800-436-8477.

2nd trimester mother

FACTS & STATS

Some women feel as if they have a constant cold with nasal congestion. This will go away after birth.

What's Happening?	Now What?
red, inflamed gums (can be pregnancy gingivitis)	• this can be caused by changes in your hormones, throughout your pregnancy, and happens if plaque is left on your teeth • to prevent this, floss and brush your teeth regularly • see your dentist and be sure to tell her that you are pregnant
little nausea, less bladder pressure, less fatigue	• the chances of having a miscarriage are very small at this stage
early milk leaking from your breasts	• wear breast pads in your bra if needed
stuffy nose and nose bleeds	• do not smoke or be around second-hand smoke • place warm, moist towels on your face for comfort • breathe steam from a hot shower, a pot of boiling water, or a vaporizer • a cool-mist humidifier may be helpful • massage your sinuses by rubbing on the bony ridge above and under your eyebrows, under your eyes, and down the sides of your nose • drink 8 to 10 cups of water a day • try saltwater nose drops made from 1/4 teaspoon of salt dissolved in 1 cup of warm water • do not use antihistamines unless recommended by your health care practitioner
quickening — the mother feels the baby's movement	• know that the feeling (e.g., bubbling, fluttering, knocking) can differ for each pregnancy • note the date, and tell your health care practitioner on your next visit
an increased sense that the pregnancy is real emotions may be more stable than in the first trimester	• pay attention to your body and baby and enjoy your pregnancy • celebrate your pregnancy • connect with your baby, and include your partner • you and your partner can talk to your baby and/or gently massage your belly • keep a diary during your pregnancy • keep a pregnancy photo album
low back pain	• maintain good posture while sitting or standing — pull in your stomach muscles, tighten your buttocks, and tuck in your seat to flatten your lower back (also see page 46) • sit in straight-backed chairs whenever possible • wear low-heeled shoes that give support • sleep on your left side with a pillow under your upper leg for support • avoid lifting heavy items • try heat or cold on your back or have someone give you a massage • consult your health care practitioner

What's Happening?	Now What?
pubic pain	• walk around objects instead of stepping over them • try not to push objects on the floor, such as boxes, with your feet • avoid opening your knees wide apart • consult your health care practitioner
throbbing of legs and appearance of varicose veins	• rest and sleep on either side with a pillow between your legs; do not lie flat on your back • walk or do other exercise • wear support hose if recommended • don't sit with your legs crossed • when sitting, do ankle and foot exercises; avoid placing a pillow underneath your knees • try not to wear knee-highs and garters • use a footrest or another chair to lift your legs when sitting
mild swelling of ankles, feet, hands, and face (edema) —may be accompanied by tingling in one or both hands	• raise your legs and feet whenever possible • lie on your left side when resting or at night to reduce pressure on major blood vessels • avoid wearing clothes or accessories that feel tight (e.g., watches, rings, or socks with elastic tops) • exercise regularly **Tips:** Swelling of your feet and ankles is normal in pregnancy. Most of the swelling should be gone when you get up in the morning. If it does not decrease with rest, talk with your health care practitioner.
hard, dry bowel movements (constipation)	• drink lots of water (8 to 10 cups per day) • if you feel your iron supplement is causing constipation, talk to your health care practitioner • eat high-fibre foods • exercise regularly • have bowel movements when you feel the urge • do not hold back or force the bowel movement • do not use suppositories, mineral oil, laxatives, or enemas unless recommended by your health care practitioner
a brownish "tan" on your face or a line running from the belly button to the pubic area	• these signs will occur in some women and disappear after the baby is born • the line from the belly button may stay there

2nd trimester mother

TEAM SUPPORT

• Enjoy feeling movements of the baby.

• Attend prenatal checkups.

• Talk to the baby.

• Gently massage the mom.

• Exercise together.

• Encourage the mother to eat a healthy diet.

• Help the mother avoid drugs and alcohol.

3rd trimester mother

TEAM SUPPORT

- Attend prenatal classes with the mother.

- Help develop a birth plan.

- Help prepare your home for the baby.

- Practice labour positions and relaxation.

- Be ready and available for labour support.

What's Happening?	Now What?
purple or red marks (striae or stretch marks) on abdomen, breasts, and thighs	• after birth, the stretch marks will gradually change from red or purple to tan or white and will become harder to see • some women never lose their stretch marks
dry, itchy skin	• if you choose to use soap, try glycerin soap • avoid long, hot baths • apply oils or lotions to keep your skin moisturized, especially after a bath or shower • calamine lotion may relieve the itching • if you have severe itching, talk with your health care practitioner
increased fatigue (feeling more tired)	• rest often and listen to your body • ask someone to help with daily chores • if possible, stop work early if you are overtired
feelings of doubt or fear about labour	• develop a birth plan • talk with your health care practitioner about concerns and plans for labour • learn about labour and birth so you know your options • attend prenatal classes
pre-labour or Braxton Hicks contractions	• these contractions are normal • tell your health care practitioner if the contractions are regular and become uncomfortable
muscle cramps in legs, especially at night	• make sure you get enough calcium in your diet or talk to your health care practitioner about a calcium supplement • avoid getting too tired • put your feet up • exercise daily • take a warm bath before going to bed • stretch your lower leg area before going to bed
feeling impatient because the pregnancy seems as though it will never end	• a full term pregnancy is anywhere from 38 to 42 weeks • call upon your support system when you feel frustrated and talk about your feelings
hemorrhoids (piles)	• avoid constipation and straining • do pelvic floor (Kegel) exercises; see page 46 to find out to how to do these • rest and sleep on either side with a pillow between your legs; do not lie flat on your back • try not to sit or stand for long periods of time — change positions or walk around • for relief, apply ice wrapped in a cloth to the area

What's Happening?	Now What?
heartburn	• eat small, frequent meals • avoid fried, fatty, and spicy foods • drink lots of liquids between meals • elevate your head and shoulders while resting • do not bend or lie down immediately after a meal • do not wear tight waistbands • chewing sugarless, non-peppermint gum (ideally containing xylitol) may also help
sudden groin pain	• avoid sudden movement • bend slightly at the hips when you expect to cough or sneeze
shortness of breath	• try taking deep, slow breaths through the mouth • wear loose clothing • use good posture • get plenty of rest

difficulty sleeping	• have regular sleep habits
	• exercise daily (take walks)
	• before going to bed try:
	  • taking a warm, relaxing bath
	  • eating a snack with a warm drink
	  • using extra pillows for support
	  • practising deep breathing and relaxation exercises
	  • listening to relaxing music

improved breathing	• make a note when this happens and tell your health care practitioner at your next visit (this usually means your baby has moved down into your pelvis in preparation for birth)
increased need to pee	• pee regularly • avoid caffeine • do pelvic floor (Kegel) exercises (see page 46)
an increase in Braxton Hicks contractions	• this is normal • your uterus is contacting to soften and thin your cervix in preparation for labour • pack your hospital labour kit (see page 57 for what to pack) • arrange to have care for your children and your house while you are in the hospital

Fetal Growth Stages

The first trimester (or first 14 weeks) is an important time in your baby's life. It's a time of fast growth and development. It's also a time when your baby is most at risk from hazards such as smoking, alcohol, drugs, infections, and X-rays.

The second trimester is the time between 15 and 27 weeks gestation. During this time your baby's brain grows a lot. The baby is still too small to live outside of your body.

4 weeks
6 mm (1/4 in.)

The third trimester is the time between 28 weeks and your baby's birth. The closer to full term or 40 weeks gestation your baby is, the better your baby is able to cope with birth and to life outside your body. Forty weeks gestation is the date estimated to be your due date.

If your baby is born before 37 weeks gestation, it is considered to be *preterm* (born early). If your baby is born after 42 weeks gestation, it is said to be *post term*. There is a higher risk of illness and death in babies born too early or too late.

Check the chart on pages 28 – 30 to follow the development of your baby.

8 weeks
22 – 24 mm (1 in.)

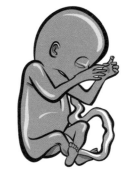

12 weeks
9 cm (3 1/2 in.)

16 weeks
16 cm (6 1/2 in.)

20 weeks
25 cm (10 in.)

28 weeks
35 – 37 cm (14 in.)

1st trimester baby

First Trimester 0 – 14 weeks

The first trimester (the first three months of pregnancy) is a critical time in your baby's life. It is the period of rapid growth and development. By the end of the first trimester, all of your baby's organs will be formed and functioning.

Time	Weight and Length	Events
1 day		The sperm and ovum unite.
7–10 days		The fertilized ovum attaches to the lining of the uterus. The placenta begins to form.
2 weeks		Your baby, called an embryo, is now a layered disc on the uterus wall. You will miss your menstrual period.
4 weeks	0.4 g (0.01 oz.)	The beginnings of the embryo's eyes, ears, nose, spine, digestive tract, and nervous system are present. The tube for the future heart starts beating.
8 weeks	22–24 mm (1 in.) 1g (0.036 oz.)	Your baby, called a fetus, now has all the organs that a full term baby will have. The heart is functioning. Bones begin to form.
12 weeks	9 cm (3 1/2 in.) 15 g (0.5 oz.)	Tooth buds are present. Fingernails and toenails are forming. Immature kidneys secrete urine to the bladder. External genitalia are forming. The fetus can now move in the amniotic fluid, but you can't feel it. Your health care practitioner may be able to hear your baby's heart beat with an electronic listening device.

Second Trimester 15–27 weeks

During the second trimester (the next three months of your baby's life) the brain develops a lot. Most of the brain's development begins now and continues for two or more years after your baby's birth. During the second trimester until about 24 weeks, the fetus cannot live outside your body because its lungs, heart, and blood systems have not developed enough.

Time	Weight and Length	Events
16 weeks	16 cm (6 1/2 in.) 100 g (4 oz.)	The face looks more human, the head has hair, the ears stand out, and your baby can hear your voice. Between 16 to 20 weeks you may feel the baby's movements. You may not feel the movements until 18 to 20 weeks, especially if this is your first pregnancy.
17 weeks		The baby begins to store some of your antibodies. This slowly increases until birth.
20 weeks	25 cm (10 in.) 300 g (10 oz.)	Eyebrows and eyelashes appear. A fine downy hair (lanugo) appears all over your baby's body and may be present at birth. Your baby's skin is thin, shiny, and covered with a creamy protective coating called vernix. Oil glands appear. Your baby's legs lengthen, and move well. Teeth develop — enamel and dentine are being formed. This can begin as early as 14 weeks. By the end of the fifth month, your baby is about half the length of a newborn. During the second trimester, meconium (the baby's first stool) begins to appear in the intestines.
24 weeks	30 cm (12 in.) 600 g (1 1/3 lb.)	Sweat glands form. Your baby has a lean body with red and wrinkled skin. Early breathing movements begin. A substance called surfactant is formed in the lungs. This substance helps the lungs to expand normally after the baby is born.
26 weeks		The baby's outline may be felt through your abdomen. The eyes may be open now.

2nd
trimester
baby

3rd
trimester baby

Third Trimester 28 weeks to birth

During the third trimester (the last three months of pregnancy) the baby could survive if born before it is full term. The earlier a baby is born, the greater the need for special care to decrease the risks from a preterm birth. The closer to full term, the more able the baby is to cope with the birth process and life outside the uterus.

Time	Weight and Length	Events
28 weeks	35–37 cm. (14 in.) 1100 g (2 lb. 5 oz.)	Your baby's body is still lean but the skin is less wrinkled and red. The baby can now store iron, calcium, and other nutrients. Your baby can hear and respond to sounds.
32 weeks	40–42 cm (16 in.) 1800–2100 g (4 lb.–4 lb. 7 oz.)	Your baby's skin is pink and smoothes out as the fat forms under it. Your baby develops a sense of taste and becomes aware of sounds outside your body. The male baby's testicles begin to drop into the scrotum. The pupils in the baby's eyes can react to light.
36 weeks	45–47 cm (18 in) 2200–2900 g (4 lb. 11 oz.–6 lb. 5 oz)	Your baby's body is rounded and usually plump. The downy hair on the baby's body begins to disappear. The skin is smooth, pink, and covered with a grayish-white cheese-like substance called vernix. The baby continues to increase the store of your antibodies and is able to resist some diseases. Usually your baby can safely be born at this age.
40 weeks	45–55 cm (18–22 in.) 3200 g + (7 lb.+)	Head hair is usually present. The testicles of male babies are now in the scrotum, and the labia majora of female babies are developed. **Your baby is now full term!**
40–42 weeks (post dates)	weight will increase	The fontanels (soft spots on the head) are becoming smaller and the skull bones are growing firmer and less flexible. The skin may become looser as the fat layer decreases. Skin is also drier and may have small cracks as the amount of vernex decreases. Nails may be long.
More than 42 weeks (Overdue)	weight will increase	The skin continues to get drier and will have cracks as the amount of vernix continues to decrease.

Medical Care during Pregnancy

Your doctor or midwife can help you have a healthy pregnancy and healthy baby. At the beginning of your pregnancy you should visit your health care practitioner every four to six weeks. After about 30 weeks you will have visits every two to three weeks. In the last month, your health care practitioner will want to see you every one to two weeks or more.

You may need extra medical attention or health care advice from your health care practitioner if you:

- are underweight or overweight
- had problems with a previous pregnancy, for example, if your baby was preterm or weighed less than 2500 g (5 lb. 8 oz.)
- have diabetes, high blood pressure, or other medical conditions
- are over 35 or under 16 years of age
- are carrying more than one baby
- have had a caesarean birth or uterine surgery
- use alcohol, cigarettes, or drugs
- are under emotional stress or there is violence in your life
- are dealing with depression or other mental health issues

Before you visit your health care practitioner, write down any questions you may want to ask. The *BC HealthGuide* handbook has two tools you can use. These are the "Healthwise Self-Care Checklist" and the "Ask the Doctor Checklist" at the front of the book. Use these to write your questions and concerns. If you don't have a copy of the *BC HealthGuide* handbook, you can request a free copy from the Ministry of Health Information Line at 1-800-465-4911.

Take important information when you visit your health care practitioner. This can be a family medical history or changes in your condition. Have your partner or support person go with you. That way, they can ask questions, hear the same information, and share in the excitement of your growing baby.

My last regular menstrual period began on _____

My last Pap test was done on _____

Our blood groups are _____

I have had:
Miscarriages   ☐ No ☐ Yes How many? _____
Stillbirths   ☐ No ☐ Yes How many? _____
Live births   ☐ No ☐ Yes How many? _____
Forceps, breech, caesarean section births
                  ☐ No ☐ Yes How many? _____

Our lifestyle risk factors include: _____

Medical conditions I have that may affect pregnancy include:

_____

I am taking these medications: _____

I am using these herbal remedies:_____

We had or have these sexually transmitted infections:

_____

I have had German measles (Rubella)   ☐ No   ☐ Yes
I have had Chicken pox (Varicella):   ☐ No   ☐ Yes

This is what we would like from our health care practitioner:

_____

We have these questions:

_____

_____

To Do

Your health care practitioner will ask you some questions during your first prenatal visit.

To prepare, take a moment to fill in the questionnaire on this page.

Tests that are usually done at all prenatal visits include:
- blood pressure and pulse
- urine test
- baby's heart rate
- measuring your abdomen to check the growth of your baby

Your First Visit

Your first pregnancy visit is usually the longest because your health care practitioner will take a detailed physical history and do a physical examination. What may be done at the first visit?

Discussion/Procedures	Why?
take a pregnancy test	• to confirm your pregnancy
take a detailed medical history	• to find any risk factors you may have
discuss lifestyle factors (use of alcohol, drugs, tobacco, exercise habits, and nutrition)	• to keep your baby as healthy as possible
discuss prenatal supplements	• 0.4 mg of folic acid daily reduces the risk of spina bifida in your baby • do not take high-dose vitamin A supplements in pregnancy • some natural herbal remedies are not safe in pregnancy
have a complete checkup that includes: • listening to your heart • taking your blood pressure • measuring your height and weight • having an abdominal examination • having a pelvic exam that includes a Pap test or vaginal swab (if not done in the last 12 months)	• to check your cervix and to check for infections
complete blood tests	• to check complete blood count (includes hemoglobin and iron levels) • to confirm blood group, Rh type, and antibody screen • to test exposure to syphilis • to screen for HIV (recommended) • to test for hepatitis • to test for rubella (German measles) antibody
complete urine tests	• to check for any sugar, protein, and urinary tract infections

Your Next Visits

What may happen on the visits that follow?

Discussion/Procedures	Why?
ultrasound test (done between 18–20 weeks)	• to check the development and position of the baby • to check the due date (you may be unsure when you had your last period)
complete a Maternal Serum Screening (also known as Triple Marker Screening) blood test (done between 15–20 weeks and is only useful when the due date is known)	• this is a blood test to help find out the risk of certain abnormalities that may affect your baby (see page 51) The test does not tell whether a baby is healthy or not. It only gives a risk factor. If the risk factor is high, further testing is done.
conduct glucose screening (done 24–28 weeks)	• checks for gestational diabetes that may develop during pregnancy This type of diabetes happens during pregnancy because pregnancy hormones change the way a woman's body uses insulin. For most women, blood sugar levels can be controlled by diet, but some women may need to take insulin by injection. For most women, gestational diabetes goes away after their baby is born.
conduct another complete blood test (done at 24–28 weeks)	• a shot of Rh-immune globulin will be given to women who are Rh-negative
take a vaginal swab for Group B Streptococcus (done at 35–37 weeks)	• Group B Streptococcus (GBS) is a type of bacteria found in the vagina and large bowel of 15 to 20% of healthy pregnant women Around the time of birth, GBS may be passed to the baby through the birth canal. If the baby gets a GBS infection, it can be serious. Because of the small chance of GBS infection in the newborn, all pregnant women should be screened at 35–37 weeks of pregnancy. A swab for GBS is taken from the vagina and anal areas. Women whose test is positive are given intravenous antibiotics, just to be safe. Often it is a brand of penicillin and is given at the time their membranes rupture or during labour. Treatment of the pregnant woman with antibiotics has been shown to decrease the chance of serious infection. However, no method has been proven to prevent all serious infections. Whether or not you need treatment in labour depends on your situation. Discuss GBS with your health care practitioner.

Your Next Visits (continued)

Discussion/Procedures	Why?
discuss your emotional feelings	• women may become depressed during the third trimester of pregnancy 10–16% of pregnant women will have depression during their pregnancy. A smaller number will also have anxiety or panic disorder.
count fetal (baby) movements (done from 35–37 weeks and onward)	• to be aware of your baby's movements Babies who are well have active periods and quiet periods during the day and/or night. Healthy babies may slow down slightly toward the end of pregnancy, but they do not slow down a lot. Your baby should not stop moving at a time when she is normally active. You don't need to record your baby's movement count unless: • you are asked to do so by your health care practitioner • you have noticed a big drop or no movement at a time when your baby is normally active To count your baby's movements: • pick a time when your baby is normally active • pick a comfortable position—semi-sitting or lying on your left side—and relax • with your hands on your abdomen, count your baby's bouts of movement—these may be a short kick or wiggle, or long, continuous squirming motion • time how long it takes for your baby to move 10 times, then record the length of time on a chart Tell your health care practitioner if your baby is moving a lot less than usual.
do a non-stress test	• tells how well your baby is doing • a painless test to check your baby's heartbeat while resting and moving • done before labour with an electronic fetal monitor

See your health care practitioner right away or call the BC NurseLine's 24-hour toll-free number at 1-866-215-4700 if you have:

- contact with anyone who has rubella (German measles) as there is a danger to your baby if you get sick with rubella during your pregnancy

- rashes of any kind except the ones you often get, like eczema

- sudden, unusual thirst

- coughing that isn't getting better

- a feeling of being tired all the time

- dizziness, headaches, dimming and/or blurring of vision

- sudden or continuing swelling of your hands or face

- frequent vomiting, when you are unable to keep fluids down

- abdominal pain or if your abdomen feels hard

- bleeding from your vagina, bowel, or bladder

- a burning sensation when peeing

- coloured, frothy and/or bad-smelling vaginal discharge, or vaginal discharge causing itchiness or irritation

- a gush or trickle of water from your vagina

- constant negative feelings or anxiety about your pregnancy and care of the baby

- depression or periods of weeping that don't go away

- any violence or threatening behaviour towards you in your home or workplace

- found that your baby has moved a lot less than usual in the last 12 hours

- signs of preterm labour (see page 80)

Share this information with your partner so you both know what to watch for.

Foods that are sweet or stick to your teeth can increase the risk of tooth decay. Remember now that you are snacking more, you need to brush more often using a toothpaste that contains fluoride.

For more information, look at BC HealthFile #38b, *Pregnancy and Dental Health* online at www.bchealthguide.org.

Eating for Pregnancy and Breastfeeding

During pregnancy you will need more calories and nutrients for your developing baby and for yourself. Don't forget that the placenta is growing and your blood supply is also increasing.

Women who eat well during pregnancy are more likely to have a baby born at a healthy weight. Eating healthy foods gives your baby the nutrients needed to develop normally. This increases your chances of having a healthy baby. You don't need to eat special foods to breastfeed, but healthy foods will keep you healthy as a new mother.

Eating Guidelines

Canada's Food Guide to Healthy Eating can help you with good eating habits. These good habits will help your pregnancy, your breastfeeding, and the rest of your life.

Remember to:
- enjoy a variety of foods from the four food groups every day
- eat three meals and two to three snacks every day
- eat foods rich in nutrients

Healthy Eating Tips
Encourage your partner and whole family to eat better:
- When families eat together, they eat better.

- Buy in bulk and share with friends.

- Nutritious foods can be quick and simple.

- Cook larger amounts and freeze leftovers for later.

- Keep convenient and healthy snacks with you so you don't go for that bag of chips or pop.

- When eating out, choose foods such as salads, chili, or pizza.

- Note the sizes of suggested servings in the *Canada's Food Guide to Health Eating*. They are often smaller than you think!

- Try not to skip meals. If nausea is a problem, try smaller meals and regular snacks.

Your community nutritionist will suggest places that can help if you have limited money. If you do not have a community nutritionist, your public health nurse, pregnancy outreach program, or other service agencies can help.

Call Dial-A-Dietitian for reliable, confidential information and advice on nutrition for yourself and your baby, during pregnancy and after.

Suggestions for healthy snacks:
- fresh fruit
- raisins and nuts
- raw vegetables
- granola bars
- crackers and cheese
- yogurt
- cereal, with or without milk
- milkshake
- peanut butter on toast
- slice of pizza

Grain Products

5–12 SERVINGS PER DAY

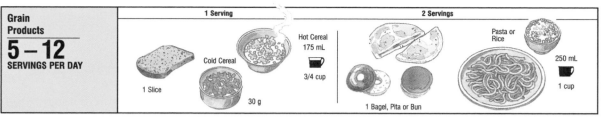

1 Serving
- 1 Slice
- Cold Cereal 30 g
- Hot Cereal 175 mL 3/4 cup

2 Servings
- 1 Bagel, Pita or Bun
- Pasta or Rice 250 mL 1 cup

Vegetables and Fruit

5–10 SERVINGS PER DAY

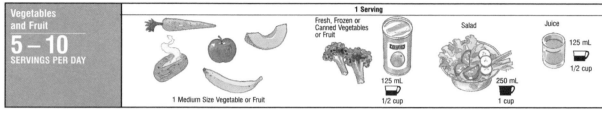

1 Serving
- 1 Medium Size Vegetable or Fruit
- Fresh, Frozen or Canned Vegetables or Fruit 125 mL 1/2 cup
- Salad 250 mL 1 cup
- Juice 125 mL 1/2 cup

Milk Products

SERVINGS PER DAY
Children 4–9 years: 2–3
Youth 10–16 years: 3–4
Adults: 2–4
Pregnant and Breast-feeding Women 3–4

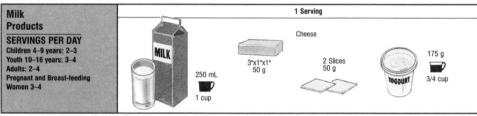

1 Serving
- MILK 250 mL 1 cup
- Cheese 3"x1"x1" 50 g
- 2 Slices 50 g
- YOGOURT 175 g 3/4 cup

Other Foods

Taste and enjoyment can also come from other foods and beverages that are not part of the 4 food groups. Some of these foods are higher in fat or Calories, so use these foods in moderation.

Meat and Alternatives

2–3 SERVINGS PER DAY

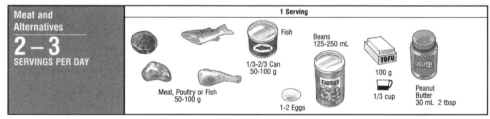

1 Serving
- Meat, Poultry or Fish 50-100 g
- Fish 1/3-2/3 Can 50-100 g
- 1-2 Eggs
- Beans 125-250 mL 1/3 cup
- TOFU 100 g
- Peanut Butter 30 mL 2 tbsp

Grain Products
Choose whole grain and enriched products.

Vegetables and Fruit
Choose dark green and orange vegetables and orange fruit.

Milk Products
Choose lower-fat milk products.

Meat and Alternatives
Choose leaner meats, poultry and fish, as well as dried peas, beans, and lentils.

Source: Canada's Food Guide to Healthy Eating for People Four Years and Over, *Health Canada, 1997.*
Reproduced with the permission of the Minister of Public Works and Government Services Canada, 2005.

Points to Remember

Take advantage of your pregnancy to work toward your goals of healthy eating. The changes you make now will set the scene for continued healthy eating for you and your baby as it grows.

A Guide to Healthy Foods

This chart shows you how to use *Canada's Food Guide to Healthy Eating* to get the nutrients you need.

Nutrient				
Iron	**Folic Acid**	**Calcium**	**Essential Fatty Acids**	**Fibre**
Benefits Needed to prevent anemia (low iron in the blood). Low iron can cause low birth weight. It can make the mother feel tired, make it hard to fight infection, and cause difficulty coping with blood loss during birth.	Lessens the risk of having a baby with neural tube defects, such as spina bifida. Folic acid is also important for healthy growth and development.	You need calcium and vitamin D for your baby's healthy bones and teeth and to protect your bones later in life.	Necessary for the normal development of your baby's nervous system and eyesight during pregnancy and breastfeeding.	Helps prevent constipation.
Grain Products bran cereal, cream of wheat, enriched cereals, wheat germ, whole-grain cereal, whole-grain bread	enriched bread and cereal, wheat germ, whole-grain bread, cereal	bread (calcium-fortified)		bran muffin, bran cereals, fibre cereal, fibre-enriched crackers, whole-grain cereal
Vegetables and Fruit apricots (dried), asparagus, broccoli, dates, prunes, raisins, spinach, Swiss chard	bananas, broccoli, romaine lettuce, Brussels sprouts, corn, beets, oranges, peas, spinach, asparagus, avocado	bok choy, broccoli, kale, mustard greens, Swiss chard		berries, dates, pears, dried figs, bananas, potatoes, prunes, kiwi, corn, peas
Milk Products Ovaltine® or Instant Breakfast® added to milk	milk, all types	buttermilk, cheese, milk, skim milk powder, yogurt, ice milk, frozen yogurt		
Meat and Alternatives tofu, baked beans, lentils, clams, dried beans, egg yolk, pumpkin seeds, meat, fish, poultry, hazelnuts, almonds, walnuts	almonds, dried beans, dried peas, lentils, peanuts, sunflower seeds, chickpeas, egg yolk, sesame seeds, hazelnuts, cashews, walnuts	almonds, baked beans, sardines, salmon with bones, soybeans, sesame, tahini, tofu made with calcium, hazelnuts	beef, pork, poultry, salmon, sardines, mackerel, walnuts, pumpkin seeds, Brazil nuts, peanuts	dried beans, dried peas, lentils, nuts, seeds

Write down everything you ate and drank yesterday.

Find the foods in the food groups in *Canada's Food Guide to Healthy Eating.*

Note below how many servings you ate of each food:

Grain Products: _____ servings

Vegetables and Fruit: _____ servings

Milk Products: _____ servings

Meat and Alternatives: _____ servings

Compare your totals with *Canada's Food Guide to Healthy Eating.*

I ate the recommended number of servings in all four food groups. ☐ Yes   ☐ No

If I ate less than the recommended number of servings in the four food groups, I need to eat more:

Grain Products _____ servings

Vegetables and Fruit _____ servings

Milk Products _____ servings

Meat and Alternatives _____ servings

How will you eat more of the foods you need?

_____

Check A Guide to Healthy Foods, page 38, and circle all the foods you ate. In which food group are you strongest? Of which nutrient group did you have the most? Of which nutrient did you get the least?

Vegetarian Eating

You need extra amounts of iron, calcium, and vitamin B12 during pregnancy. It may be hard to get these nutrients if you only eat vegetarian choices of food. Talk with your health care practitioner or a registered dietitian about supplements.

Iron

Vitamin C helps with iron absorption. Combine iron-rich foods with vitamin C-rich foods, such as berries, citrus fruits, peppers, broccoli, or tomatoes.

Calcium

Milk products are a good source of calcium. If you do not eat or drink dairy products, increase these calcium-rich foods in your diet:
- enriched soy or rice beverages
- enriched orange juice

For other non-dairy sources of calcium, see the BC HealthFile #68e, *Food Sources of Calcium and Vitamin D* at www.bchealthguide.org. The calcium in non-dairy sources is less easily absorbed than the calcium in milk.

Vitamin B12

Vitamin B12 is found in milk and eggs. Your developing baby needs vitamin B12 for brain and nervous system development. If you do not eat these foods, you should have your vitamin B12 level checked by your health care practitioner. Make sure you take a supplement containing vitamin B12—at least three micrograms per day. Some nutritional yeast contains vitamin B12, but during pregnancy and breastfeeding it is best to make sure you get enough by taking a supplement.

He Said

The best practice I got at being a parent was to try doing everything I normally did, but I did it while holding a bag of sugar in one arm.

Caffeine

Caffeine is found in many products, including coffee, tea, chocolate, cola beverages, and soft drinks. Caffeine is also in some prescription and non-prescription medications. A small amount of caffeine should not harm you or your growing baby. While you are breastfeeding, caffeine may make your baby restless.

It is recommended that you limit your intake of caffeine to about 300 mg a day while you are pregnant or breastfeeding.

- One cup of regular coffee has 135 to 179 milligrams (may vary according to the brew).

- One cup of tea has 43 milligrams.

- One 355-millilitre can of cola has 36 to 46 milligrams.

You can cut down on your intake of caffeine if you:
- replace your usual caffeine drinks with water, milk, or fruit juices
- make only one cup at a time
- change your coffee time into a time for going for a walk

Herbal Teas

It is recommended that you use herbal teas with caution. Some herbal teas are safe to have during pregnancy and others are not. Choose herbal teas that list the ingredients. Teas made from edible food products are generally safe. These herbal teas are thought to be safe: ginger, lemon balm, rosehip, blackberry fruit (not leaf), raspberry fruit (not leaf), and strawberry fruit (not leaf).

- Some herbal teas may aggravate allergies.

- Limit herbal teas to two to three cups per day.

- Call Dial-a-Dietitian for additional information on teas. (See the Resources section at the back of the book for contact information.)

Essential Fatty Acids (EFA)

Essential fatty acids are needed so your baby's nervous and visual systems can develop normally. EFAs are important for normal growth and development during pregnancy and breastfeeding. The amount of EFA needed increases during pregnancy because as your baby grows, he requires more. EFA can be found in fish, walnuts, and vegetable oils, such as canola and soybean. It can also be found in non-hydrogenated margarines and salad dressings made from canola or soybean oil.

Taking Supplements

It is important to tell your health care practitioner what types of supplements you are taking. Remember to include any herbal supplements or remedies or natural vitamin products that you use. Taking too much of any supplement may be harmful to your baby. This includes natural or herbal products.

Prenatal Supplements

Your health care practitioner may recommend a vitamin and mineral supplement made for pregnancy. This is called a *prenatal supplement*. A healthy diet and these supplements will give you the extra vitamins and minerals you need for your growing baby. It is important to take them every day. If you can't afford prenatal supplements, check with your local health office. There may be a prenatal program that provides these supplements at no cost.

Folic Acid

Take a folic acid supplement or a prenatal vitamin supplement with 0.4 to 1 mg of folic acid every day. For more information, see BC Healthfile #38c, *Pregnancy and Nutrition: Spina Bifida and Folic Acid* at www.bchealthguide.org.

Iron

Your health care practitioner may recommend that you take an iron supplement and eat foods that are extra high in iron. For more information, see BC HealthFile #68c, *Iron and You* at www.bchealthguide.org.

- An iron supplement is best absorbed if taken between meals with a light snack.

- An iron supplement may cause nausea if taken on an empty stomach.

- Take an iron supplement with foods high in vitamin C. These include berries, citrus fruits, peppers, broccoli, or tomatoes.

- Do not take an iron supplement with tea or coffee, and do not take it with foods that are high in calcium or with your calcium supplements. See page 38 for a list of foods high in calcium.

- An iron supplement may cause constipation. If constipation is a problem, see page 23.

Vitamin A

High levels of vitamin A can harm your baby. Do not take extra supplements that contain vitamin A during pregnancy or breastfeeding. Prenatal supplements have safe levels of vitamin A for pregnant and breastfeeding women.

Calcium

- Your health care provider may recommend a calcium supplement along with foods that are extra high in calcium.

- Calcium is best absorbed when taken **with** food.

- Do not take bone meal or dolomite because you can't be sure they are good sources of calcium.

- See BC HealthFile #68e, *Food Sources of Calcium and Vitamin D* at www.bchealthguide.org.

Food Safety

Some foods can carry bacteria or parasites that may make you sick. Some can affect your baby too. Follow these safety guidelines.

How can I practice food safety?

- Wash your hands well with soap and warm water after going to the toilet, and before and after preparing food. If you touch raw meat, wash your hands well before handling other foods.

Points to Remember

Always store vitamin and iron supplements safely out of reach of young children. This is to avoid poisoning.

- Wash raw vegetables well. Use a brush to remove visible soil.

- Be careful with raw and cooked foods. Keep uncooked meats and seafood separate from vegetables and other ready-to-eat foods.

- Do not put cooked foods on cutting boards or plates that were used for raw meat.

- Do not let raw or cooked foods sit at room temperature. The general rule is no longer than a total of 2 hours.

- Keep hot foods **hot** (60°C) and cold foods **cold** (4°C).

- Do not eat undercooked meat. Thoroughly cook these foods until their internal temperatures are as shown:
  - all poultry (74°C)
  - egg products (63°C)
  - meat dishes (68°C)

- Reheat food really well, to an internal temperature of 74°C.

- Use only pasteurized milk and milk products.

- Avoid eating raw fish.

- Avoid or cook well:
  - soft cheeses such as brie, feta, Camembert, blue veined, and Mexican-style cheese
  - deli meats, hot dogs, and refrigerated pâtés
  - previously cooked seafood and smoked fish

- Wash and sanitize utensils and cutting boards after handling uncooked foods. To sanitize, use 1 teaspoon of household bleach in 1 litre of water.

- Cooked foods should be refrigerated and used promptly.

- Do not keep food in the refrigerator for more than 2 days.

- Keep cooking tools and surfaces clean.

- Never leave food in open cans. Store food in covered containers.

- Check for safety seals.

- Change dishcloths and towels daily.

For more information call the BC NurseLine or Dial-a-Dietitian. See Resources at the back of the book for phone numbers.

Pet Safety

If you have contact with your cat's feces (poop), you can get a parasite that can cause a serious infection, called *toxoplasmosis*, in your unborn baby. This can result in miscarriage or birth defects. The disease is often mild or without symptoms and can be mistaken for the flu.

How can I practice safety with my cat?
- Have someone else empty the cat litter box, or wear gloves and wash your hands well.

- Wear gloves and avoid direct contact with garden soil that may have cat feces in it.

You should wash your hands with soap and water for 15 seconds after handling your pets.

Weight Gain in Pregnancy

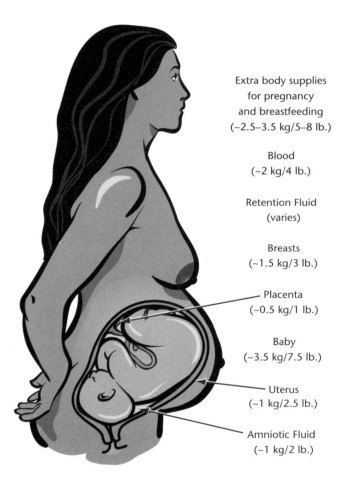

Extra body supplies
for pregnancy
and breastfeeding
(~2.5–3.5 kg/5–8 lb.)

Blood
(~2 kg/4 lb.)

Retention Fluid
(varies)

Breasts
(~1.5 kg/3 lb.)

Placenta
(~0.5 kg/1 lb.)

Baby
(~3.5 kg/7.5 lb.)

Uterus
(~1 kg/2.5 lb.)

Amniotic Fluid
(~1 kg/2 lb.)

Typical pregnancy, weight gain approximately 14 kg (30 lb.)

How much weight you should gain depends on what your weight was before you became pregnant. Underweight women need to gain more and overweight women should gain less. Weight gain is usually between 6.8 to 18 kilograms (15 to 40 pounds.) Your weight gain should be gradual. If you gain more than 3 kilograms (6.5 pounds) in a month, you need to see your health care practitioner. If you gain less than 1 kilogram (2 pounds) a month in the last six months of pregnancy, talk to your health care practitioner and review your eating habits.

If you are gaining too much weight, look at *Canada's Food Guide to Healthy Eating* and review your eating habits. You may be eating the wrong kinds of foods or too much food, or not getting enough exercise. Talk with your health care practitioner or registered dietitian for information on weight gain.

Do not diet during pregnancy. Focus on nutrition, not weight.

What about cravings?
Cravings for non-food items, such as ice, clay or starch, can usually be stopped with a change in your diet. Report any of these cravings to your health care practitioner.

To Do
The changes I plan to make to my eating habits are:

_____

_____

_____

_____

Reasons to stop exercise and consult your health car provider
- excessive shortness of breath
- chest pain
- painful uterine contractions (more than 6–8 per hour)
- vaginal bleeding
- any "gush" of fluid from vagina (suggesting premature rupture of the membranes)
- dizziness or faintness

Source: Physical Activity Readiness Medical Examination for Pregnancy (PARmed-X for pregnancy) © 2002, used with permission from the Canadian Society for Exercise Physiology, Inc. http://www.csep.ca/forms.asp

If you have any of the above symptoms, stop exercising right away and call your health care practitioner or the BC NurseLine toll-free at 1-866-215-4700.

Exercising

If you are gaining more weight than recommended, check *Canada's Food Guide to Healthy Eating*. Also, try to get more exercise.

Staying active during pregnancy will cut down on swelling, leg cramps, fatigue, shortness of breath, backache, and constipation. It will also help you keep your weight down.

What are good exercises to do while pregnant?
- walking
- riding a stationary bike
- swimming
- yoga, aquafit, prenatal exercise classes
- low-impact aerobics

How can I start an exercise routine?
- Begin exercising three times a week. Slowly increase to four times a week.

- Start exercising for 15 minutes at a time with rest breaks. You shouldn't exercise for more than 30 minutes without a rest break.

General Guidelines
- Exercise with someone. Make the activity fun and something you'll keep doing after the birth.

- Drink water or juice before, during, and after exercise.

- Eat a snack one to one-and-a-half hours before exercising.

- Warm up before exercising and cool down afterwards. How? Take 10 to 15 minutes to stretch, then do relaxation exercises or mild aerobics before and after exercise.

- If you become short of breath, stop the activity.

Safety
- Your ligaments are more relaxed now, so you can be injured more easily. Avoid bouncing and fast changes in direction, which includes games such as squash or racquetball.

- It is much easier to lose your balance when you are pregnant so be careful while doing new exercises that require balance. Don't do exercises that might make you fall and hurt your abdomen. These include contact sports, such as rugby and karate, downhill or water skiing, hockey, horseback riding, and softball.

- Do not become overheated. If you exercise in a pool, the water should not be higher than 26 to 28°C.

- Don't exercise flat on your back after the fourth month of pregnancy. The weight of your baby presses on your major arteries and veins and can reduce the blood flow to you and your baby. Put a small pillow under one hip to shift the weight of the baby off your arteries.

- Breathe throughout an exercise, breathing out on exertion and breathing in when you relax. Do not strain while holding your breath. This will cause changes in your blood pressure and can also create pressure on your pelvic floor and abdominal muscles.

- Do not scuba dive when pregnant. The fetus is not protected from decompression sickness (the bends) and gas embolism.

- Use low weights and high repetitions if doing strength training. Use lower weights as you get closer to your baby's birth.

- Don't overdo it. Pregnancy is a time when you need a balance of rest and activity.

Checking Posture

Your centre of gravity may shift forward as your uterus and breasts get bigger. This can cause a sway or arch in your lower back, and this sway can cause your shoulders to slump forward. Poor posture can cause discomfort in your back, shoulders, and hips.

Check your posture throughout the day by:
- pulling in your abdominal muscles — think "belly button to back bone"
- pulling your shoulders back and straightening your spine
- standing up straight and walking tall

Caring for Your Back

Back pain is common later in pregnancy. Follow these tips for back safety and comfort:
- keep good posture
- don't lift heavy objects
- lift with your legs and not your back, by bending your knees
- hold the object you are lifting close to your body
- do not twist when lifting
- keep your knees slightly bent but not locked when standing
- "log roll" when getting up from a lying position (turn onto your side and push up with both arms)
- rest and sleep on your side and put a pillow between your knees to support the upper leg
- avoid moving large objects
- if standing for long periods of time, put one foot on a stool
- wear comfortable, supportive shoes

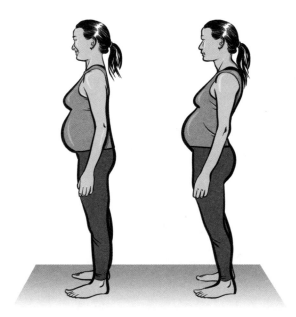

Correct posture   *Incorrect posture*

Strengthening Your Back

Strengthen your back with this exercise:

- Kneel on your hands and knees with elbows slightly bent.

- Keep your back flat. Do not let your back sag downwards.

- Keep your head and neck in line with your spine.

- Arch your lower back and at the same time tighten your abdominal muscles and buttocks.

- Slowly relax and return your back to the flat position.

- Repeat up to a maximum of 5 to 8 times.

Pelvic tilt exercise for strengthening your back.

Caring for your Abdominal Muscles

Abdominal muscles take most of the pressure of the growing baby during pregnancy. These muscles run up and down from your chest to your pubic bone. It is common for these muscles to soften, weaken, and separate, like a zipper opening under stress. If you notice bulging along the middle of your abdomen when you get out of the bath or bed, you could have a separation in your abdominal muscles.

You can lessen strain to these muscles by:

- getting out of bed by turning onto your side and pushing up with both arms
- avoiding exercises where you curl up
- not holding your breath when you lift and carry something

Until the gap is closed you should not do sit-ups and exercises that rotate the trunk, twist the hips, or bend the trunk to one side. Refer to page 47 for information on how to see if you have a separation in your abdominal muscles.

Strengthening Your Pelvis (Kegel Exercises)

Kegel exercises help to strengthen the vaginal and perineal area — the area between the vagina and anus. These muscles support the weight of your growing baby, and they also help you control passing urine and stool. Doing Kegel exercises during pregnancy and after the birth will help you strengthen these muscles, which will prevent you from leaking urine when coughing or laughing. Kegel exercises can be done anywhere.

Here's how:

- Tighten the muscles around your vagina and anus, as if you were stopping the flow of urine. Do not do Kegel exercises by actually stopping your flow of urine when on the toilet. This can cause some urine to stay in your bladder.

- Hold the muscles tight for a count of 5 and work up to a count of 10. Repeat 5 to 10 times.

- Do this exercise often throughout the day.

- Do not hold your breath while tightening your muscles.

- To prevent leaking urine, try tightening your pelvic floor muscles before you cough, sneeze, or lift.

Exercising after Baby

Exercising will help you regain muscle tone, lose weight, and have more energy. After a vaginal birth, most exercises can be started again as soon as you are comfortable. Start slowly, then gradually build up the length of exercise. If you have heavier and brighter bleeding after exercise, you need to slow down. After a caesarean birth, exercise can be started when you are comfortable and have discussed your exercise plans with a physiotherapist or doctor.

You can begin Kegel exercises a day after a vaginal birth. Let pain be your guide. These exercises will help strengthen and tone the area around your vagina, and will help you control peeing. Make Kegel exercises a regular part of your daily routine for the rest of your life.

Exercise can be a time for you, your partner, and your baby to spend together. Choose an activity that is comfortable for all of you, and make it one that easily fits into your daily schedule. If you feel pain while exercising, stop and rest.

Separation of the Abdominal Muscles
Before starting an exercise program after birth, check to see if you have a separation in your abdominal muscles by doing this test:
- Lie on your back with your knees bent and feet flat on the floor.

- Lift your head and shoulders off the floor, keeping your chin tucked in.

- Place your hand flat along the middle of your stomach, fingers pointed towards toes. You may feel a gap between the bands of stomach muscles. Note if there is any bulging in the middle of the abdominal muscles.

- If you have any bulging or gaping in the middle of your abdomen, talk with your health care practitioner.

Good Exercises
- Walking — gradually increase the pace and distance. Use a good stroller or soft carrier so you can take your baby with you. If you jog or walk quickly, wear a supportive bra.

- Swimming — you can begin swimming after vaginal bleeding and discharge have stopped.

- Postnatal fitness classes — your community may have classes designed for new mothers.

- Yoga — start slowly or join a class that is designed for new mothers.

Exercising and Breastfeeding
Exercise does not affect the amount or quality of your breast milk and will not affect the growth of your baby if you are breastfeeding. Rarely, in some women, intense exercise will cause an increase in lactic acid in breast milk and the baby may not like the taste.

If your baby does not feed well after you have done intense exercise:
- slow down
- feed your baby before exercising
- express breast milk before exercising to give to your baby after you exercise
- try feeding again a little later

Remember — your milk is still good for your baby.

Pregnancy can be a time of great stress, both physically and emotionally. I found the greatest stress reliever was learning to say **no**. That and prenatal yoga! Free your life of extra stress and find an outlet to release the stuff you just can't get rid of. Remember that by taking care of yourself, you are taking care of your baby.

TEAM SUPPORT

- Listen to your partner's concerns. You may not have solutions but you can listen and try to understand.

- Ask what you can do to help.

- Talk about your worries and concerns with someone you trust.

- Talk about how you will manage your finances.

- Join a prenatal class to learn about becoming a parent.

- Create a birth plan together.

- Talk about maternity and paternity leaves.

- Laugh together.

Reducing Stress

Some stress is normal but too much stress can be unhealthy for you and your baby.

Here are some tips for managing stress:
- talk with a professional or someone you trust
- learn to say no to extra responsibilities
- make time for yourself everyday
- exercise daily
- get enough sleep and eat healthy foods
- practice relaxation breathing
- plan ahead
- prepare your other children for the new baby
- plan when to leave work
- arrange for help in your home after the baby is born
- attend prenatal classes to learn about pregnancy, birth, and parenting

If you have a sudden crisis, such as the death of a loved one, loss of a job, or move to a new home, talk with your health care practitioner or public health nurse. You can also call the BC NurseLine at 1-866-215-4700 for advice about seeking professional help.

To Do

My top two de-stressing activities are:

_____

_____

I will fit these two (or more) activities into my life by:

_____

_____

_____

Travelling

What about car travel?

Wear your seat belt with the lap belt below your baby and the shoulder belt against your chest.

Always wear seat belts in the car. Wear the seat belt as shown to protect yourself and your baby if you are in a crash.

- Wear the lap belt snug and low over your pelvic bones, below the baby.

- Wear the shoulder belt tightly against your chest.

- Do **not** put the shoulder belt under your arm or behind your back.

- Do **not** recline your seat while travelling because your seat belt will be too loose to protect you.

- Do not be the driver if you don't have to be. If you do drive, adjust the vehicle's front seat as far back as you can. This will give the air bag as much room as possible in which to inflate if you are in a crash.

Reproduced and adapted with permission from the Insurance Corporation of British Columbia

What about air travel?

Before you buy a ticket, check with the airline about their policy on pregnant travellers. Some will not allow you to fly after 36 weeks gestation. They may also require a letter from your health care practitioner that includes your due date.

If you are flying while pregnant:
- ask for an aisle seat so you can get up and walk frequently
- drink plenty of water
- bring your own healthy snacks
- keep your medications with you on the plane

If you are travelling a long distance:
- take a copy of your prenatal record
- find out about health care in the area you are travelling to
- find out the location of the nearest hospital
- take out medical insurance that includes pregnancy and birth

Also talk with your public health office about immunizations. Discuss any precautions you should take to prevent illness while travelling. These include drinking bottled water and staying away from ice cubes and uncooked fruits and vegetables.

Sexuality

There may be changes in your sexual relationship, but it is possible for a couple going through pregnancy and parenthood to have an intimate relationship. Pregnancy may be a time to experiment. Find comfortable activities that please both of you.

Is sex during pregnancy safe?

Normally, sex does not harm the baby. However, if intercourse is painful, talk with your health care practitioner.

Are there some situations when we shouldn't have sex?

Most couples can have sex right up until active labour. Your health care practitioner may advise you to avoid vaginal intercourse if you have conditions such as:
- the placenta is over the cervix (placenta previa)
- the bag of waters has broken
- the cervix is opening early
- there is a history of preterm labour before or during this pregnancy

Even if you have been advised to avoid intercourse, there are many other ways to have an intimate and loving relationship with your partner.

Will desire change in pregnancy?

Both women and men experience a change in their level of interest in sex during pregnancy. Some will find they have an increased desire for sex. Others will not.

Women may find their breasts and vulva are more sensitive and orgasms are more intense. Other women find they are too tired and nauseated, and have to struggle to adapt to their changing bodies. Some partners may not want to have sex, thinking it may harm the baby or start labour.

He Said

I didn't realize how stressed I had been about becoming a dad until I was talking with my brother. I just started crying; it was crazy. I had been worried about money, losing my job, would I be a terrible dad, would I faint during the birth, would I basically make a mess of the best thing that had ever happened to me? Would I...? Would I...? Just hearing that he had felt some of the same things really calmed me down.

Tips for Having Sex

- Uncomfortable? Try positions you do not normally use, and use pillows to help support where needed. When the baby has engaged in the pelvis, the woman can try lying, crouching, or kneeling with her back to her partner so he enters her from behind.

- Too tired? Try the morning, afternoon, or a time when you are more rested.

- Breasts leaking? Try wearing a padded nursing bra.

Tips for Partners

Use questions to keep communication open:
- Is this position still comfortable for you at this stage?
- What can I do to make this better?
- Does this hurt?
- Are you worried about the baby?
- Would you like to try something else?

Check in frequently during sex to be sure your partner is comfortable and enjoying the experience.

What about orgasm?

A mother's orgasm can trigger the uterus to contract. This can happen even with masturbation or oral sex. However, this usually does not affect the baby. Contractions normally stop after a few minutes. If you have a risk for preterm labour, you may be advised by your health care practitioner to avoid orgasms during your pregnancy.

Is oral sex OK?

Oral sex can be an alternative to vaginal sex. Two points to remember are:
- Don't let your partner blow air into your vagina because it can cause an air bubble in your blood stream. This is a very serious complication.

- Do not have oral sex if your partner has a cold sore (herpes virus) because the virus can infect you.

Will sex start labour?

Not unless you are ready to go into labour already or are at risk for preterm labour.

If your baby is due, sex may help your body get ready for labour because:
- Semen contains a hormone called prostaglandin that may help start contractions and soften the cervix.

- Stimulation of the nipples by rubbing, rolling, or sucking releases the hormone oxytocin. This can also cause the uterus to contract. You will notice these as after pains when you first start breastfeeding after birth.

- Orgasm can cause the uterus to contract.

How soon after the baby is born can we have sex?

You may have sex again when you feel ready, usually when vaginal bleeding has decreased and any tears or stitches have healed. It is normal for women to need time to "get in the mood." Feeling well rested and lots of foreplay will help. Vaginal dryness can make intercourse uncomfortable, but using a sterile, water-soluble lubricant in the vagina and/or on the penis can help. Before you start having sex again, ensure you have effective birth control.

Working Safely

Talk to your health care practitioner about any risks at work, such as dangerous chemicals and fumes. Also talk about infections or if you get overheated at work. You may have to stop doing physical work, such as heavy lifting, during your pregnancy. Talk to your boss about job changes during this time.

Be comfortable at work. If you stand for long periods:
- shift your weight from one foot to the other often
- put one foot on a footrest
- wear comfortable, supportive shoes
- have as many breaks as possible and try to find a quiet place to lie down or at least put your feet up

If you sit for long periods:
- change your position often
- use a footrest
- get up and walk as often as possible

Pregnancy Risk Factors

Mid-life Pregnancies

Pregnant women over 35 are considered to be of advanced age. What are the risks of pregnancy over 35?
- Increased risk of having a baby with a disease or condition that is inherited. Because it is carried through the genes, this is known as a genetic abnormality.

- Greater chance of complications with the pregnancy. Examples are diabetes, high blood pressure, and caesarean birth.

- Increased risk of miscarriage.

Age is less important than:
- a woman's health
- nutrition
- lifestyle
- medical and family history
- having good medical care

What do I do if an abnormality is found?
- Most tests are normal. If there is an abnormality, a counsellor or your health care practitioner will talk with you about your options.

Genetic Counselling

If you wonder about your chances of having a healthy baby, you can talk with your health care practitioner about genetic counselling. If you meet with a genetic counsellor, you and your partner may both be asked to have blood tests. If you are 35 or older, amniocentesis will be offered.

What about testing?

Sometimes a fetus may not be developing normally. Often medical procedures or tests can determine this before the baby is born. Talk to your caregiver so you can compare the possible risks and benefits of having these tests. You can read more about the following tests on BC HealthGuide OnLine at www.bchealthguide.org.

Maternal Serum Screening (Triple Marker Screening)

Maternal Serum Screening is a blood test for pregnant women who have been pregnant for 15 to 20 weeks. It screens for woman who have a greater risk of carrying a baby with Down Syndrome (a chromosome abnormality). This test also checks for open neural tube defects, such as spina bifida.

This test measures the amount of three markers in the mother's blood. The test does not determine whether or not a baby is affected. It only gives a risk factor. If the risk factor is high, further testing is done. If you are considering Triple Screen testing, see the BC HealthGuide OnLine at www.bchealthguide.org for more information.

I was scared about the amniocentesis. The thought of that long needle going into my belly just made me sick. While it was being done, I was amazed at how little it hurt. To tell the truth I didn't realize the needle was in until I saw it on the ultrasound screen.

Amniocentesis

This diagnostic test finds genetic abnormalities, such as Down Syndrome, and it is very accurate. Amniocentesis is usually done between 15 and 18 weeks. A needle is used to remove a small amount of amniotic fluid through the mother's abdomen. This test is done with ultrasound guidance. You will have to wait one to three weeks for the results. There is a small risk of miscarriage with this procedure.

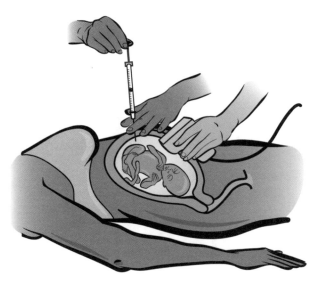

Amniocentesis

Chorionic Villus Sampling (CVS)

CVS is used to detect genetic abnormalities. This diagnostic test can usually be done between 11 and 13 weeks of pregnancy. A small amount of tissue (chorionic villi) is removed through the vagina or the abdomen with a needle. You will usually know the results by 13 to 16 weeks.

Medical Complications

Gestational Diabetes

This form of diabetes can develop during pregnancy. It usually goes away after birth. For most women, following a diabetic diet and getting regular exercise can control this condition. Some women with gestational diabetes will need to manage it with insulin injections. Your doctor, in consultation with a registered dietitian or diabetes educator, can help you manage gestational diabetes.

Vaginal Bleeding

A small amount of vaginal bleeding in the first trimester does not mean you are having a miscarriage, but vaginal bleeding in the second and third trimester should be considered serious. If you have vaginal bleeding any time in your pregnancy, stop whatever you are doing and talk to your health care practitioner.

What your caregiver needs to know if you have vaginal bleeding:

- What colour is it? Pink, brown, or red?

- When did it start?

- What were you doing when it started?

- How much is there? For example, is it spotting the size of a quarter, or soaking your underwear?

- Did it happen after intercourse or a vaginal examination?

- Are you having cramps, pain, or any other symptoms?

Placenta Previa

With placenta previa, the placenta is either partially or completely blocking the cervix. This condition may cause vaginal bleeding. If you have a placenta previa at the time of birth, a caesarean birth will be recommended.

High Blood Pressure

High blood pressure is also known as Pregnancy-Induced Hypertension (PIH). It can lead to toxemia and pre-eclampsia. About 7 in 100 pregnant women will develop high blood pressure. If it is not treated, it can harm both you and your baby.

Signs of high blood pressure in pregnancy:
- swelling in your hands and face
- rapid weight gain
- unusual headaches that don't go away
- blurred vision
- spots or stars in front of your eyes
- pain in the upper right side of your abdomen

Immediately contact your health care practitioner or the BC NurseLine, at 1-866-215-4700, if you have any of these symptoms.

Premature Rupture of Membranes (PROM)

PROM is when the bag of water — also called amniotic sac or membranes — breaks or leaks before you are in labour or before your due date. The type of treatment will depend on:
- how many weeks pregnant you are
- how much fluid was lost
- whether you develop an infection

If your membranes break or leak:
- use a sanitary pad
- note the colour and amount of the fluid
- contact your health care practitioner
- do not take baths, put in a tampon, or have sex

Breech Position

By about 32 to 36 weeks, most babies will move into the birth position. This is usually head down, meaning that the largest part of the baby is born first. In the breech position, the baby's buttocks or legs are facing down and will be born first. There are risks when you have a breech birth. Your health care practitioner will probably recommend a caesarean birth.

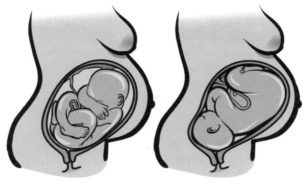

Breech presentation   *Head down presentation (97% of babies at birth)*

Rh Factor and Blood Type

Blood tests will tell your blood type and Rh factor, but there is no way to find out your baby's blood type until after birth. If you are Rh-negative and your baby is not, you could develop antibodies — similar to having an allergic reaction — to your baby's Rh-positive blood. This can happen if your blood and your baby's blood mix at birth, during an amniocentesis test, or if bleeding occurs in your pregnancy. This can cause serious illness or even death for your next baby. Because it can be prevented, it is seldom seen today. If you are Rh-negative, you will receive an injection of Rh-immune globulin (RhIg). This will prevent your body from forming antibodies and causing possible harm to your next baby.

The RhIg will be given:
- at about 28 weeks gestation
- after birth if your baby is Rh-positive
- after an amniocentesis
- if you have any vaginal bleeding

Preparing To Give Birth

In British Columbia, women and their partners can choose where to have their baby — in a hospital with a doctor or midwife, or at home with a midwife. Doctors in BC are not permitted to do home births.

You may be advised to have your baby in a hospital if:
- you are carrying more than one baby
- your baby is in a breech position (bottom down) or other unusual position
- you have early labour before 37 weeks, or late labour after 42 weeks of pregnancy
- you have a medical condition, such as high blood pressure, heart or kidney disease, or diabetes
- you have active genital herpes
- you have had a caesarean birth before
- you have a high-risk pregnancy for any other reason

To Do

It's important that both you and your partner are comfortable with the place where you choose to have your baby.

When thinking of birth choices, ask:
- Where will we feel safe and be able to relax and focus on my labour?

- Am I in good health, without any medical problems in my pregnancy?

- Where can my health care practitioner attend the birth?

- Will my partner and I be involved in the choices about my care?

Health Care Support

While you are pregnant you will get medical care from your midwife or family doctor. You may have special needs, such as carrying more than one baby, or you may have a medical condition, such as diabetes or heart or kidney disease. If this is the case, your doctor or midwife may ask an obstetrician to give you medical care. An obstetrician is a doctor trained to care for women who have special needs during their pregnancies and birth. If needed, an obstetrician may also be called during your labour and birth.

Having your baby at home?
You need to get medical care from a midwife if you plan to have your baby at home. Your midwife will be with you during your labour. A second birth attendant will also be present for the birth of your baby. She will be there for a short period of time before and after your baby's birth. Until six weeks after the birth, your midwife will give information and care as you need it. This help is for you and your baby and includes breastfeeding support.

After the birth, your midwife will see you or contact you at home on a daily basis for a week. At two weeks, you will return with your baby to your midwife's office for visits until six weeks after your baby's birth. At that time your care will be transferred back to your family doctor. You will receive information from a public health nurse about services from the health office and services in your community.

Having your baby in a hospital?
A nurse and your midwife — if you have one — will be with you during your labour and birth. Your doctor will usually check on you during labour and will be with you during the birth of your baby.

After you go home you will be contacted and visited as needed by a public health nurse. She will answer questions about your baby's feeding and care. She will also talk with you about your health and postpartum adjustment. She will give you information about services provided by the health office and about other services in your community.

The public health nurse is not available after office hours and on weekends or statutory holidays. During these times, call the BC NurseLine, at 1-866-215-4700, for confidential health information and advice from a registered nurse.

Personal Support

During labour and birth you can choose to have your partner and anyone else you want to be with you. Having someone with you and your partner during labour has been shown to lessen the amount of pain medication needed and to shorten labour. Before your baby's birth it is helpful to decide who you want to be with you. Many women choose their partner and other important people, such as a close friend, relative, or parent to be with them. Some women also choose to have a doula. A doula provides emotional and physical support to you and your partner before, during, and just after birth. A doula does not provide medical care. The cost of a doula is not covered by the Medical Services Plan.

Because your labour may be longer than you expect, it may be helpful to have more than one person with you. Then they can take short breaks if needed and you will not be alone. For more information on pregnancy care and who can help, see the pregnancy topic in BC HealthGuide OnLine at www.bchealthguide.org.

What about children?
Can my other children be at the birth?
Yes, children can usually be there. Talk to your health care practitioner about this ahead of time. You will need to have someone look after your child. If your child needs to leave the room, the support person can look after her. The person who looks after your child should be someone other than the people who are providing your labour support.

Your Birth Plan

A birth plan is a written outline of the things you would prefer to do or have happen during your labour, birth, and the days following birth. It can be a useful tool for you and your support team as you work together. During your prenatal visits, talk to your health care practitioner about the things you would like, but be aware that for a number of reasons, it is not always possible for every part of a birth plan to be followed.

There are many reasons why you may want to write a birth plan:

- To inform your doctor, midwife, and nurses at the hospital what you would prefer to happen during your labour and birth. Examples include walking as much as possible or having no medication unless asked for. Other examples are being in a semi-sitting position for the birth or touching your baby's head during the birth.

- To inform your doctor, midwife, and the nurses at the hospital what you would prefer to have happen if your labour or birth needs medical help. For example, being awake for a caesarean birth.

- To inform your care providers about the care you would prefer for your baby after birth, such as holding your baby skin-to-skin.

- To help you and your support team work together.

- Your birth plan is just that — a plan. Be flexible. Sometimes things happen that you cannot control and your plan has to change.

- A short plan — about one page — is easiest for everyone involved in your care to read.

She Said

We didn't do a birth plan this time. We had one when our daughter was born and I felt like a failure as our birth changed so much from what we had initially planned. We had wanted a natural birth, soft lights, and no painkillers. As it turned out the baby was in a posterior position so I had a back labour all through the night. By the morning I was exhausted and asking for an epidural. I ended up with an epidural, IV, monitor, and six people in the room. We were still delighted with our daughter but had this written proof that things went wrong. This time we are just going to go with the flow and do the best we can with the kind of labour we get and be happy with a healthy baby.

Birth Plan for: Kim and Tom Lee
Due Date: October 2nd
Doctor: Dr. Goodforyou

What we prefer for labour and birth:

- My support people will be my partner Tom, my mother Peggy, and my friend Heather. I would like them to stay with me during my labour and birth.

- We would like to walk around during my labour and spend as much time in the shower as possible.

- I would like to drink water and juice during labour. I do not want an intravenous unless it is necessary.

- My goal is to avoid drugs, except perhaps Entonox near birth, if I ask for it. I would really like your ideas and support for non-medical ways to manage pain.

- Please help Tom in his efforts to help me.

- We would like to have music playing during labour. We will bring a CD player.

- I would like to push squatting or semi-sitting when I have the urge, not with coaching.

- We would like to have a mirror in place to see the birth.

- I would rather have a small tear than an episiotomy, and neither if possible.

- After the birth, we would like to have the baby placed up on my chest, unbundled and skin-to-skin.

- Tom would like to cut the umbilical cord.

- I would like to breastfeed our baby as soon as possible after birth and continue breastfeeding on cue.

- I know babies feed frequently at night and I want to feed on cue without supplements. Help us breastfeed frequently and find ways to settle our baby.

- If I am overwhelmed with visitors, help me remind them that I need to rest.

If things do not go the way we hope they do:

- If I have a caesarean birth:
  - I would like to be awake and have Tom with me.
  - All other plans for our baby would remain the same.

Sample birth plan

Packing for the Hospital

Have your things prepared before you go into labour. Pack a small bag; you may be in hospital for only 24 to 36 hours and personal storage space is limited. Place the things you will need for labour at the top of your bag or in a separate bag. If you are planning a home birth, your midwife will give you a list of the supplies you will need to prepare.

Here are some ideas for what to take to the hospital.

Labour Kit:
- *Baby's Best Chance: Parents' Handbook of Pregnancy and Baby Care*
- lip balm or lip gloss
- massage oil or talcum powder
- snacks and drinks for you and the support team
- partner's swimsuit, so he or she can get into the shower with you
- camera, film
- CD player or tape player (with headphones) and some music
- a picture, a design, a figure, or anything you find pleasant to look at
- list of friends' and family's telephone numbers
- slippers
- dental care products
- hair care products
- skin care products
- other personal items
- coins for phone calls

Personal Items:
To be brought in after the baby is born.
(Note: your clothes should be loose fitting and comfortable.)
- washable dressing gown (front-opening for breastfeeding)
- two or three nightgowns or pairs of pajamas (front-opening for breastfeeding)
- nursing bra and pads, if desired
- at least three pairs of panties
- socks
- comfortable bedroom slippers
- large sanitary pads
- clothes to wear home

For the Baby:
- Canadian Motor Vehicle Safety Standards (CMVSS) approved infant seat
- undershirt and sleepers
- diapers, pins, and plastic pants or disposable diapers (newborn size)
- sweater, bonnet, and booties (if wearing a gown)
- shawl or blanket, depending on the weather
- soft carrier or sling to use to help calm your baby

For the Partner:
- sleeping bag or bedding and pillows for partner (hospitals usually only supply the sleeping mat)
- sweat pants and top suitable for sleeping

TEAM SUPPORT

I promise that:
- This birth will be the priority for my time and energy.

- I will make sure everyone at work knows I may have to leave on short notice.

- I will have gas in the car or have other transportation arranged ahead of time.

- I will not plan important travel or events for two weeks before and two weeks after the due date.

- I can be reached at any time.

- I will have child care arranged for any children who will **not** be attending the birth.

- I will have arranged child care for any children who will be attending the birth.

- I will be kind, supportive, encouraging, and helpful.

The start of Michelle's labour was pretty confusing. She was awake all Sunday night with contractions that kept her awake but then fell asleep again in the morning and everything stopped. The contractions started up again and she walked to try to keep it going. All day it was off and on. She was awake most of Monday night with contractions and a little bit of show. She sent me to bed, thank goodness. Again it stopped when she had breakfast and a bath. On Tuesday we went to the hospital exhausted, and our son was born late that night.

Preparing for Labour

What is the difference between pre-labour and true labour?

It is easy to confuse pre-labour with true labour. Contractions may be uncomfortable in both true and pre-labour. Although both may be uncomfortable, there are clear differences between them. If you are less than 37 completed weeks in your pregnancy, you may be in preterm labour. See page 80.

What should we do if we're not sure of pre-labour or labour?

- If it's night, try to sleep. You want to be well rested for childbirth. In true labour you may not be able to sleep but will at least rest. If you fall asleep, it is most likely pre-labour.

- Take a shower. The contractions in pre-labour will often become less frequent and shorter. In true labour the contractions will continue no matter what you are doing.

- Distract yourself. Watch a movie, walk in the garden, play cards. If you are in true labour, the contractions will demand your attention. If it's pre-labour, you may be able to carry on with your usual routines.

Pre-labour	True labour
• Contractions are at irregular intervals, e.g., every 5 to 15 minutes.	• Contractions occur at more regular intervals, e.g., 5 to 10 minutes apart.
• Contraction length varies, e.g., lasting 20 seconds to 90 seconds.	• The length of contractions usually increases, e.g., lasting 30 to 60 seconds.
• Although they may be painful, the strength of contractions remains the same or may lessen.	• Intensity of contractions gradually increases, becoming progressively more painful.
• Contractions are often felt in the lower abdomen.	• Contractions can be felt in the abdomen, across the lower back, and sometimes in the thighs
• You may find that contractions are most uncomfortable when you are moving and lessen when you are resting.	• Contractions do not decrease when you are resting, but continue regardless of what you are doing.
• The cervix usually remains closed.	• The cervix thins and shortens (effaces) and opens (dilates).
• There is usually no "show" (blood-tinged mucus).	• There may be "show" and/or leaking from your bag of waters.

When should we call our health care practitioner or hospital?

- When your contractions are regular and painful, last 30 to 60 seconds, and happen at 5-minute intervals.

- If your bag of waters breaks.

- If you have vaginal bleeding or show.

- If you are unsure and have concerns.

- If your health care practitioner has advised you to call early.

- If your baby stops moving or moves less than usual.

- If you're not sure and can't reach your health care provider by phone, call the BC NurseLine at 1-866-215-4700. That way you can speak with a registered nurse who can give you helpful information and advice when you need it most.

Relaxing for Labour

Learning to relax can help with childbirth and the busy time after your baby is born. Remember; try to relax, stay positive, breathe through your contractions, and rest between them.

Here are some relaxation and breathing techniques you can use. Practice all the techniques well before you go into labour, so you know which will be the most helpful to you when labour begins. If possible, practice the techniques with the person who will be with you during the birth.

Focal Point Concentration
Being able to focus on something other than pain can help you relax. This is true even when you are having a contraction. During labour you may want to look at something or someone and try to clear your mind.

Visualization
Picture something or some place that makes you feel relaxed and safe.

Water Therapy
Stand or sit in the shower and direct the water to where it feels comfortable. A warm bath can also be relaxing. Don't take a bath if your bag of waters has broken and you are leaking amniotic fluid.

Massage
Use smooth, rhythmic stroking or rubbing of the face, neck, shoulders, back, thighs, feet, or hands. Do it yourself or have someone give you a massage.

There are three types of massage:
- light, rhythmic stroking of your abdomen
- squeezing and releasing
- pressing with the hand on the lower back to relieve backache

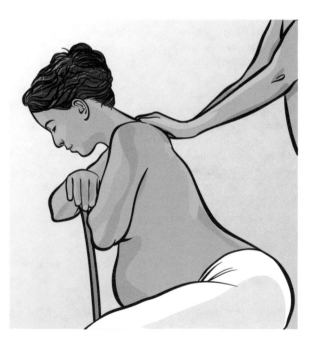

Labour is like getting ready for a marathon. You need to be prepared. If you have practiced comfort positions, relaxation, breathing techniques, and other rituals, you will be able to choose the ones you find helpful. While in labour you will need to pace yourself and rest whenever possible. Drink fluids to keep hydrated. Use comfort positions as well as breathing techniques to help with relaxation.

Complete Relaxation

You can do this exercise alone or with your partner:

- Tense and relax each part of your body in turn, using moderate tension, for a period of three to five seconds. (Tensing too strongly can cause muscle cramps.)

- Breathe in as you tense and out as you relax. Focus on how good it feels each time you relax.

- Work from your toes to the top of your head.

Breathing for Labour

During labour, breathing techniques or variations of them can be used to:
- help with relaxation
- focus your attention during a contraction
- maintain a good supply of oxygen to yourself and your baby
- help relieve pain

Practice a variety of breathing techniques before labour. This will help you to use and change them as needed during labour. They will help you be calm and relaxed.

When you cannot remain relaxed or walk or talk during a contraction, you may wish to use slow breathing for as long as it is helpful. Then you may wish to change to light breathing. You may find that you use both or only one of these breathing techniques. You will also adapt them to suit your needs.

Slow Breathing

- Breathe in slowly through your nose, or through your mouth if your nose is congested.

- Breathe out through your mouth, letting all the air out like a relaxing sigh.

- Breathe about half your normal rate.

- Try to keep your shoulders dropped and relaxed.

Light Breathing in Labour

- Let your contractions guide you in the rate and depth of your breathing.

- Breathe in and out through an open mouth. Breaths will be shallower than slow breathing.

- Breaths will be about twice your normal rate.

- When a contraction starts to decrease, return to your slow breathing.

- When the contraction ends, take a deep breath and end with a relaxing sigh.

- Try to completely relax, change your position, or have a sip of fluid as desired.

Short Breath Holding

- During the second stage of labour, you may feel the impulse to push down with each contraction.

- The number of pushing (bearing down) efforts increases as the baby moves down the birth canal.

- You may push down with some short breath holding (usually lasts less than 6 seconds).

- If you have an epidural, you may have a delayed, lessened, or loss of the urge to push.

Panting

During the second stage, you may be asked to use panting breaths. This helps you control the urge to push and allows the baby's head to come out slowly and gently.

- Lift your chin.

- Have your mouth open slightly.

- Breathe in and out lightly and quickly (like a dog panting).

Comfort Positions during Labour

For comfort, walk, move, and change your position as often as you can. Try to stay upright, relaxed, and moving as much as possible to help move your baby down in your pelvis. These positions may help you to manage pain and avoid medications. Your partner can stay involved and supportive by helping you move and change positions often.

Walking (1st Stage of Labour)
- Being upright moves the baby's head down in your pelvis. It also helps to relieve backache.

Standing (1st Stage of Labour)
- Rock or sway the hips and lean forward while standing.

- Leaning forward and resting on something while standing can be restful and relieve backache.

- To relieve backache, try counter pressure. Counter pressure is firm, constant pressure applied to the back where pain is localized. This can be from a partner's hand or leaning against a firm object, such as a rolled towel, tennis ball, or wall.

Sitting Upright (1st and 2nd Stages of Labour)
- Sitting on a toilet may help relax your bottom for pushing.

- Can be a restful change from standing and can be used if you have electronic fetal monitoring.

- If your hemorrhoids and backache are more painful in this position, stand up and move around.

Semi-sitting (1st and 2nd Stages of Labour)

- Semi-sitting can be a restful position. You may be able to nap between contractions.

- If you lean forward and rest on your partner, it is easier to have your back rubbed.

Birthing Ball (1st and 2nd Stages of Labour)

- Have someone help you stay balanced. Don't use a birthing ball if you are slippery with oils or lotions.

- Balls are useful to lean on when you are in a kneeling position or to sit on if you have someone to help you keep your balance.

Kneeling (1st and 2nd Stages of Labour)

- Doing the pelvic tilt can take pressure off hemorrhoids and relieve backache. See page 46 to see how to do the pelvic tilt.

- To lessen the strain on your hands and wrists, lean forward on a chair or bed.

- While you kneel and lean on a support, have someone give you a massage or use counter pressure. Counter pressure is firm, constant pressure applied to the lower back where pain is localized. A partner's hand or a firm object, such as a tennis ball, can be used to apply pressure.

Side-lying (1st and 2nd Stages of Labour)

- Alternate between lying on your side and walking during the first stage of labour.

- This position is comfortable during birth if your upper leg is well supported so you can relax between contractions.

- It is a safe position if you have taken medication for pain or have an epidural.

- It takes the pressure off hemorrhoids.

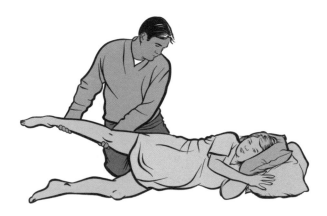

Squatting (1st and 2nd Stages of Labour)

- This position takes advantage of gravity and widens the pelvis to help the baby come down and out.

- It makes your legs tired, so change positions between contractions.

- Your partner can wrap his arms around you, either from the front or back. You can lean on your partner while squatting.

Giving Birth

Most women want to know how long their labour will be. A normal labour can be anywhere from three hours or less to days. The average length of time for a woman giving birth for the first time is 10 to 14 hours once contractions are regular.

There are four stages to labour and birth. First stage is labour, second stage is pushing, third is delivery of the placenta, and the fourth is the first few hours after birth.

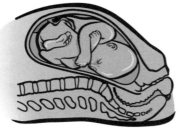 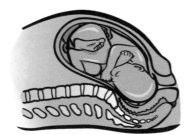 

1st Stage: Effacement and Dilation

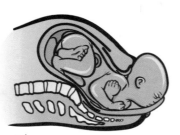 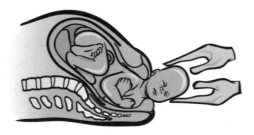

2nd Stage: Birth

3rd Stage: Placenta Expulsion

4th Stage: Skin-to-skin Contact

The four stages of labour

TEAM SUPPORT

- Listen to the mother. She can tell you what she needs.

- During labour, actively support her. Make eye contact, say "Breathe with me," and do the breathing yourself so she can follow you. At the end of contractions say, "Take a deep breath and relax."

- Help her to stay relaxed by touching, massaging, talking, breathing with her, and reminding her to move around. Check for relaxation by touching her arms, shoulders, and legs.

- When a contraction starts, focus on her. If people are trying to talk to her, let them know she is having a contraction. If you find it helpful, you can time the contractions. That way you can tell her when a contraction is at its peak and when it should be easing off.

- When a contraction is over, give her sips of fluids and help her to move and relax.

- Talk and encourage her. Give verbal encouragement by saying, "You're doing great. The contraction is almost over." When the contraction ends, say, "Take a deep breath and relax. It's over."

- If the she tells you something is not working for her, do not try to force her to follow you. Move onto another relaxation or breathing technique that may be more effective.

- Tell her she is doing well. Make eye contact and smile.

- Tell her not to worry about any noises she makes— many women find making noise helps them get through the pain of their contractions.

- Get ice chips, wipe her forehead, walk with her, rub her back, and help her with comfort positions.

- Have her eyeglasses with you so she can watch her baby being born.

- Stay with her.

- Try to stay calm.

- Take care of yourself—bring snacks and something to drink.

- Talk to the doctor, midwife, and the nurse about your birth plan.

- Ask questions if you have any concerns or don't understand something.

Any time the mother needs help to cope, you may need to take charge for a while. To take charge:

- Move in close and have your face near hers.

- Be calm and say encouraging things.

- Hold her shoulders or head in your hands. Hug her tightly but gently.

- Tell her to open her eyes and look at you. Make eye contact.

- Encourage her with every breath and say things like, "Breathe with me, stay with it, look at me, good for you, it's going away now." Use a calm and confident tone.

- Talk with her between contractions and ask if you are helping. You might say, "Let's breathe together. You are doing great. Let's get through this part together. Let me help you more this time."

- Don't give up when she says she can't go on. Tell her it is hard now but that you can do it together, this is normal, and think of the baby to come. It is OK to ask for help.

- Stay with the mother during labour.

- If you are unsure of what to do, ask the health care practitioner to give you some ideas.

Fetal Monitoring

During active labour, your baby's heart rate will be listened to every 15 to 30 minutes. This will tell your health care provider about the effects of the contractions on the baby's heart rate. This is done using a hand-held stethoscope called a Doppler. In the second stage, your baby's heart will be listened to every five minutes or after each contraction. In some situations, there may be a need to monitor your baby's heart with a machine called an electronic fetal monitor.

There are two types of electronic fetal monitoring:
- External: two sensors will be placed around your abdomen.

- Internal: a clip will be placed through the cervix onto the head of your baby.

First Stage

The first stage is the longest stage of labour and is focused on opening the cervix to allow your baby to pass during birth.

The first stage has three phases: early, active, and transition. It begins with contractions that continue to increase in length and intensity, and ends when the cervix is fully opened. The early or latent phase is the very early part, when the cervix opens to 3 to 4 centimetres. During the active phase, your cervix opens from about 4 centimetres to 8 or 9 centimetres. In the transition phase, the cervix opens the last 1 to 2 centimetres.

The first stage can last from a few hours to days. The length of this stage will depend on how strong and often your contractions are and the position of your baby.

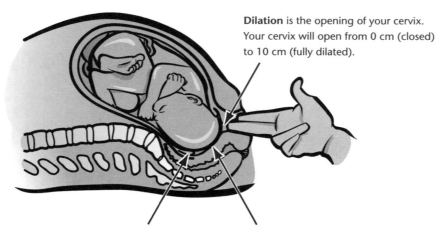

Dilation is the opening of your cervix. Your cervix will open from 0 cm (closed) to 10 cm (fully dilated).

Effacement is the thinning and shortening of your cervix. It usually happens before you start to dilate.

Station is the position of your baby's presenting part (lowest part) in relation to your pelvis.

Checking the amount of dilation during the 1ˢᵗ stage of labour

1st stage labour

Early First Stage

What is happening?	What might you be feeling?	What can you and your support person do?
• Your cervix is opening to about 3–4 centimetres and is softening. • The baby's head is coming down in your pelvis. • You may have some diarrhea. • You may notice "show" (slightly pink, mucusy vaginal discharge). The mucus plug normally sits in the cervix. As the cervix opens, the plug falls out. • Your bag of waters (membranes) may leak or rupture. This can happen any time before or during labour. You may have a small trickle or a big gush.	• Backache and pelvic pressure, as if your period is starting. Some women will feel discomfort in their thighs, hips, and abdomen. • Contractions may feel like mild cramps and may last about 20–45 seconds. • Contractions may not be regular. They may start every 10–20 minutes, or you may not be aware of them at first.	• Carry on your usual activities as long as possible. Go for a walk, try to sleep or rest, make meals. • Breathe in a normal manner until you can no longer talk or walk through contractions, then start with slow breathing as needed. • Eat a light meal and remember to drink fluids. • Take a shower if someone is nearby. Try to postpone having a bath until you are in active labour, unless you are very tired. Baths may slow or stop your contractions temporarily when taken in early labour. Do not have a bath if your membranes have ruptured. Later in labour, having a bath is very helpful because it can help decrease the pain and increase your labour progress. • If your membranes rupture, put on a sanitary pad and call your health care practitioner. • If your membranes rupture and the amniotic fluid is green go to the hospital. Green amniotic fluid means that your baby has had a bowel movement (meconium). This may happen for no reason. It may also happen if your baby has been stressed or is in a breech position.

Call your health care practitioner or hospital when:

• Your contractions are regular and uncomfortable, usually about 3–5 minutes apart and lasting 45–60 seconds.

• Your bag of water breaks or leaks.

• You have vaginal bleeding, more than show.

• You are uncomfortable staying at home.

• You have been advised to call for other reasons.

Active First Stage

What is happening?	What might you be feeling?	What can you and your support person do?
• Contractions may be moderate in strength. They may come every 3 – 5 minutes and last 45 – 60 seconds.	• Serious, quiet, and thinking mostly about yourself and your labour.	• Use positions that are most comfortable. Try to keep moving between contractions. If you are tired, rest between contractions.
• Show may become heavy, dark, and bloody.	• In need of quiet support.	• Use relaxation techniques, such as visualization, focal points, massage, touch relaxation, or TENS (see page 75).
• Your cervix continues to open.	• Wondering if you can cope with contractions.	• Continue slow and light breathing or using breathing techniques that you like.
• Your baby's head continues to move down in your pelvis.	• Contractions will be stronger and more uncomfortable.	• Concentrate on one contraction at a time. • Sip fluids between contractions or suck on ice chips.
• Your health care practitioner will listen to your baby's heartbeat every 15 – 30 minutes or more often if necessary.		• Pee frequently. • Have a warm shower while sitting on a chair or leaning on your partner.

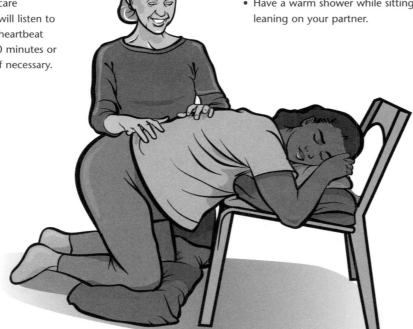

1st stage labour

TEAM SUPPORT

- Tell her she is almost done and everything is going well.

- Wipe her forehead with cool cloths.

- Offer small sips of fluids between contractions.

- Look her in the eyes and help her to focus during contractions.

Transition Stage

What is happening?	What might you be feeling?	What can you and your support person do?
• Your cervix is now almost fully dilated.	• Moments of panic and confusion.	• You need a lot of support during transition.
• The baby moves down further into your pelvis. This puts pressure on your bottom.	• More and more irritable, sensitive, and having trouble saying what you need.	• Picture your cervix and body opening up to let your baby out.
• Contractions may be strong. They may come every 2 – 3 minutes and last 60 seconds.	• Some nausea and vomiting. • Leg cramps.	• Tell someone if you have the urge to push. • If you have the urge to push and you are not fully dilated (10 centimetres) use panting until you are fully dilated.
• Your health care practitioner will listen to your baby's heartbeat every 15 – 30 minutes.	• Trembling of arms and legs. • Hot or cold flashes. • Constant discomfort with no relief between contractions. • Sweating on your face. • A strong urge to push with contractions.	

Second Stage

During the second stage of labour you will push your baby out. Second stage begins with full dilation and ends with the birth of your baby. This stage can last from a few minutes to two to three hours.

What is happening?	What might you be feeling?	What can you and your support person do?

• You will have a vaginal examination to be sure you are fully dilated. If you push too soon the cervix can become swollen and difficult to open further.
 	
• Once your cervix is fully open, your baby is pushed out.
 	
• If your bag of waters has not broken already it may be broken to help you along.
 	
• Your baby's head pushes against your perineum.
 	
• Your baby's heartbeat will be checked every 5 minutes or after every contraction.
 	
• Your baby's head is usually facing your spine.
 	
• As your baby's head first emerges, it will slip back into your vagina between contractions.
 	
• Your vagina stretches to allow your baby to pass through.
  • your perineum may not tear at all
  • you may have a small tear of the perineum
  • you may have an episiotomy (cut in the perineum) to allow more room for your baby's head
	• Contractions will be powerful and pushing the baby out. They will come about every 2–3 minutes and last 60–90 seconds.
	
	• You may feel a strong urge to push.
	
	• You may go through a short time with no contractions and no urge to push.
	
	• You will have a splitting and burning feeling on your perineum or vagina as they stretch.
	
	• Surprised, overwhelmed or frightened by the pushing sensation.
		• Breathe deeply.
		
		• Relax your bottom and go with the urge to push.
		
		• If you feel better grunting with contractions and giving small pushes go with this urge.
		
		• Use the same muscles to push that you would use for a bowel movement.
		
		• Drop your chin towards your chest and relax your tongue.
		
		• Get into your birthing position (e.g. semi-sitting, squatting, kneeling or side-lying). Support people can help hold your legs, or support you as you squat.
		
		• Continue with relaxation techniques between contractions.
		
		• Listen to your body and use the breathing techniques you practiced.
		
		• If you are asked to stop pushing, use the panting breathing technique.

2nd

stage labour

2ⁿᵈ stage labour

Second Stage (continued)

What is happening?	What might you be feeling?	What can you and your support person do?
• As your baby's head crowns (the largest part of the head is birthing) you may be asked to stop pushing. This allows the head to come out slowly and helps prevent tears.	• Very tired but feeling a burst of energy.	• After the baby's head is born, you may be asked again to stop pushing for a moment so your health care practitioner can check if the umbilical cord is around your baby's neck. Use the panting technique.
• When your baby's head is out, it is usually face down but will turn to one side. Mucus in the baby's nose and mouth may be suctioned out.	• Anxious and hesitant to push due to pressure on your bottom.	• You may be able to touch and stroke your baby's head before the body is born.
• With the next contraction your baby's shoulders and body will come out.	• Like you are having a bowel movement (you may pass some stool as you push).	• Look at your baby being born, either by looking down or having a mirror in place.
	• Full of emotion at the birth of your baby.	• Your baby will be placed on your chest.

Third Stage

During the third stage, the uterus contracts. The placenta completes its separation from the wall of the uterus and is birthed. This stage can take 5 to 30 minutes or longer.

What is happening?	What might you be feeling?	What can you and your support person do?
• The umbilical cord will be cut and clamped after the baby is born.	• You may have cramps as the placenta comes out.	• Cuddle with your baby on your chest.
• Just after birth a health care practitioner will take an Apgar score. This checks your baby's overall health.	• You may be asked to push out the placenta.	• If your partner wants to cut the umbilical cord, he or she will be given scissors and told where to cut.
• The placenta separates from the wall of the uterus and is pushed out the vagina.	• You may feel relieved, grateful, and filled with joy. Some mothers don't have any particular feelings at this time.	• Bring your baby to your breast to begin breastfeeding. Some will suck right away; others will take a little while.
• The uterus rises in the abdomen and takes on a grapefruit shape and size.	• Exhausted.	• Warm blankets will be put over you and your baby to keep your baby warm.
• A gush of blood often comes with or before the placenta comes out.	• Shaky and cold.	• If asked to, give small pushes to push out the placenta.
• You may be given a shot to stimulate contractions of the uterus and stop you from bleeding too much.	• Hungry and thirsty.	• Talk to your baby. He already knows the sound of your voice.
• If you have had a tear or episiotomy, the area may be frozen and stitched.	• Focused on the baby and wanting to know that your baby is normal.	

3rd stage labour

He Said

It was amazing when our son was born. He was put right up onto my wife's chest, all slippery and wet. I had to hold onto him so he didn't slide off. Even before the placenta was out he was rooting round for the nipple. So my wife moved him over a bit and he latched on right away. I think the breastfeeding really helped because as soon as he was nursing, my wife had cramps and the placenta was delivered.

4th stage labour

The birth of our baby was the most amazing thing we have ever experienced. It was hard work for my wife but she was so strong and in control. I was in awe of her. The moment we first held our daughter will be forever etched in my heart. I'm a pretty tough guy but it brings tears to my eyes just thinking of it.

Fourth Stage

The fourth stage is the first two or three hours after birth.

What is happening?	What might you be feeling?	What can you and your support person do?
• Your body is recovering from the hard work of labour and birth.	• Tremors and chills.	• Ask for more warm blankets as you need them.
• Your baby may breastfeed or nuzzle your breast.	• Discomfort from after pains, episiotomy or tears, and hemorrhoids.	• Place an ice pack (wrapped in a towel) between your legs to decrease swelling in your perineal area.
• You have lost blood during the birth and you may be very tired.	• Dizzy or faint if you try to get up.	• Drink fluids and have a light meal if you are hungry.
• Your body may begin to shake.		• Have help before you get up.
• Difficulty peeing due to swelling.		• Continue breastfeeding and cuddling your baby.
		• Keep your baby skin-to-skin for as long as you wish. Skin-to-skin is the best way to keep your baby warm. Partners can help keep baby warm skin-to-skin if you need to get up.

Medical Procedures that May Be Needed to Assist Labour and Birth

Sometimes interventions may be needed for you or your baby during the birth process. The most common are outlined below. You may wish to discuss these with your health care practitioner ahead of time.

Induction

Induction of labour is used to start labour before it begins on its own. It can be done by:
- breaking the water bag around the baby
- putting a gel into the vagina
- giving medication by IV to start contractions

Induction may be considered if:
- the mother is one to two weeks past the due date
- the mother has an illness, such as heart disease, diabetes, or high blood pressure
- the baby is not growing well

Episiotomy

An episiotomy is an incision (cut) made in the area between the vagina and rectum. This cut enlarges the space for the baby to pass through the vaginal opening. Freezing is usually given first. After the placenta comes out, the cut is sewn shut with self-dissolving stitches.

Forceps

Forceps are instruments that are placed around the baby's head and used to gently help pull the baby out. They can leave red marks or slight bruises on the baby's head, but these soon fade. An episiotomy may be done before forceps are used.

Forceps are used if:
- the mother has a prolonged pushing stage of labour
- the mother is exhausted and unable to push effectively
- the baby's heart rate slows showing signs of stress
- the position of the baby's head needs to be changed

Vacuum Extraction

A soft plastic vacuum cup is sometimes used to assist with birth. It is put on the baby's head and suction can then be used to help pull the baby out. The cup can leave a bruise and swelling on the baby's head, but this will fade a few days after birth.

A vacuum is used if:
- the mother has a prolonged pushing stage of labour
- the mother is exhausted and unable to push effectively
- the baby's heart rate slows showing signs of stress

Pain Relief Options

Labour pain is different for every woman. Many women cope with pain with the help of:
- a supportive person
- breathing techniques
- relaxation
- warm baths
- showers
- changing positions
- massage and/or visualization
- ice packs
- acupressure
- hypnosis

Transcutaneous Electronic Nerve Stimulation (TENS) can be used for relief of back pain. Four electrodes are placed on the lower back. They are attached to a small, hand-held battery device. The woman adjusts the stimulation. The stimulation gives tingling, buzzing, or prickling sensations over the back.

Pharmacological Options

Sometimes women in labour need additional pain relief. This table outlines some options for pain relief medications during labour and birth.

Pain Relief Option	Benefits	Side Effects
Nitrous Oxide and Oxygen (Entonox) Commonly known as *laughing gas*.	• Can be used right up until birth with no effect on the baby. • The woman in labour holds the face mask and breathes in the amount she requires.	• Only recommended for 2–3 hours. • May make some women feel dizzy and have temporary tingling or numbness in their face or hands. • Will only dull the pain, but will not take the pain away.

Narcotic Pain Medications (such as Demerol, Fentanyl)	• Can be given by a health care professional by one of two routes:
	  • Intramuscularly (IM) — the medication is injected directly into a muscle.
	
	  • Intravenously (IV)—the medication is injected directly into a vein.
	
	 • Most given by IM will work within 20–30 minutes and will last 2–4 hours.
	
	 • Most given by IV will work within 2–3 minutes and will last 1–2 hours.
	
	 • These time frames may vary depending on the medication.
	
	 • In general, narcotic medications will make most women feel sleepy and relaxed.
		• May make the baby sleepy. If a narcotic is given near birth, it may affect the ability of some babies to breathe and breastfeed.
		
		 • Usually given before the late part of the first stage of labour due to its effect on the baby at birth. This way, it can wear off before the baby's birth.
		
		 • May make some women feel drowsy, dizzy, or nauseated.
		
		 • Will only dull the pain, but will not take the pain away.

Pain Relief Option	Benefits	Side Effects
Epidural/Spinal Local anaesthetic is injected into the space around the spinal cord, providing pain relief from the waist down. During a caesarean birth, pain relief is from the breastbone down.	• Used at any time during labour. • Provides the most effective pain relief. • Women in labour can have more medication if needed. • May be used for a caesarean birth so women can be awake during the birth. • Women generally do not feel drowsy or groggy.	• Women may have to stay in bed as they will not have good control of their legs. • Women may shiver at first and may itch from the medication. • Blood pressure will be checked frequently. • Most women will also need to have an intravenous (IV) during an epidural. • Women usually have a fetal monitor during an epidural, which may restrict movement. • Women may have a catheter inserted into their bladder to drain urine. • Women may not feel the urge to push or be able to push well. • Increased risk of forceps delivery. • Pain relief may not be complete. • Some women have a headache after an epidural.
Pudendal Block Local anaesthetic is injected to numb the nerves around the vagina. This blocks pain in the vagina, vulva, and perineum.	• May be given at the time of birth.	• May affect the ability of some babies to breastfeed immediately after birth.
General Anaesthetic Completely asleep during caesarean and birth.	• Is used when an epidural or spinal is not possible or unsafe to give. • Is used when there is not enough time to place an epidural. • Is used in an emergency situation.	• A woman may react to anaesthesia or other medications during the surgery. This can be dangerous to her health. An example of a reaction is her blood pressure dropping quickly. • Her throat may feel dry and sore after the anaesthetic. This is due to the breathing tube placed in her windpipe while she's asleep. • She may feel nauseated and vomit after surgery.

Caesarean Birth

A caesarean section (or C-section) is the birth of a baby through a cut in the abdomen and uterus. Your doctor may recommend a caesarean birth to protect you or your baby. A caesarean can be done before or during labour.

When would I have a caesarean birth?

- The cervix does not open completely.

- Labour is not progressing.

- The baby is too big to fit through the mother's pelvis.

- The baby is in distress (not tolerating labour well).

- Multiple pregnancy (twins or triplets) in which the babies are in difficult positions.

- The baby is in a breech (bottom or feet first) or transverse (sideways) position.

- The mother has a serious medical condition.

- The mother has active herpes lesions on her genitals that make vaginal birth unsafe for the baby.

- The mother has had a previous caesarean birth.

What are the choices for an anaesthetic?

- The most desirable anaesthetic is an epidural or spinal anaesthesia. When you have these, you are usually awake and alert during the surgery and birth. Most hospitals allow your partner in the operating room if you are awake.

- If you have had an epidural or spinal anaesthetic, you will be able to cuddle your baby skin-to-skin. In some hospitals you may be able to put your baby to the breast soon after birth.

- If you have a general anaesthetic, you will be completely asleep during the surgery and birth. Your partner will not be allowed in the operating room but can usually hold the baby very soon after birth.

What happens after a caesarean birth?

- Pain medication will help you move around more easily. You will probably need it for several days. Ask for it when you need it.

- You will have an IV in your arm until you are drinking well.

- You will have a catheter — a tube into your bladder to take away the urine — until you are able to get up to the bathroom.

- You will be getting out of bed within 24 hours after the birth. You will need to have help the first few times you get up.

- The surgery will not affect breastfeeding.

- If you had staples, they will need to be removed. If you have sutures (stitches), they will usually dissolve by themselves. If you have small adhesive strips across the incision and they do not fall off within a week, carefully peel them off.

- You may have a shower or tub bath as desired.

- You will need help at home. If you try to return to your usual activities too soon, you will slow your recovery. Healing may take six weeks or longer.

- Don't lift anything that weighs more than your newborn baby. If you have toddlers, sit down and have them climb up on your knee.

- You will need to heal from major surgery as well as the birth of your baby.

- You can resume driving when you feel well enough, are able to twist your body to look to each side, and can quickly use the foot pedals in an emergency situation. (Similar to before you were pregnant.)

- Eating healthy foods and drinking lots of fluids will help you heal.

What about breastfeeding?

You will need to experiment to find the most comfortable way to feed your baby. If you hold the baby across your abdomen, try to prop your baby well above your incision. Many women find lying on their side comfortable. This position works better if you have someone to help latch your baby. The football position may also work (see page 99).

What about future births?

Most women who have had a caesarean birth can have a vaginal birth for their next pregnancy. You should be offered a "trial of labour" or an attempt to have a vaginal birth if:
- your hospital has timely access to do a caesarean birth if needed
- your pregnancy is normal
- the reason you had a caesarean before no longer applies
- the incision you had before is across your uterus, not up and down

The worry with a vaginal birth after a caesarean is that the scar on the uterus may pull apart during labour and cause bleeding. This is a rare complication. Your health care practitioner or nurse will ask if you have constant abdominal pain during labour, heavy vaginal bleeding, dizziness, or faintness.

If you want to learn more about vaginal births after a caesarean (VBAC), go to BC HealthGuide OnLine at www.bchealthguide.org. Search the database for "Caesarean Birth."

Vaginal Births Versus Caesarean Births

Some people may think a caesarean birth is easier and less painful than a labour and vaginal birth. Caesarean births are quick but they do have risks.

If you have a caesarean birth, you will have:
- a greater chance of infection
- a higher risk of complications to you and your baby from the anesthesia
- a longer hospital stay
- fewer support people with you at the birth
- a longer recovery time
- pain from the surgery

If you're afraid of a long and painful labour, talk to your health care practitioner. You may want to consider having additional support during your labour and birth. This could be a doula, who can provide support to both you and your partner. Pain relief is available during labour if you need it.

To Do
In your birth plan, include your thoughts and feelings about your choices related to caesarean births. You may need to talk to your health care practitioner about what you would like.

Our daughter was born at 34 weeks gestation by caesarean section. My wife had really high blood pressure and the baby was being stressed. I watched her heart beat going down with every cramp. It was a very scary thing for both of us. I had to leave the operating room because my wife was having a general anesthetic, which was the fastest way to get the baby out. I didn't know if I would see a live, healthy baby come out of that room or not. It turned out she was very small, but healthy. She did need to stay in the special care nursery for a few weeks though. I'd have to say that was one of the most frightening things we have ever gone through.

Special Birth Issues

Preterm Labour

Preterm labour is labour that begins before 37 completed weeks of pregnancy. Preterm labour can happen to anyone and it is often not known why. Preterm labour may result in your baby being born too soon.

Preterm babies are at higher risk of:
- breathing difficulties
- sucking and swallowing problems
- jaundice (yellowish skin)
- infections
- bruising and bleeding
- problems maintaining body temperature
- longer hospital stays

The earlier your baby is born before term, the greater the risk of developing lifelong problems, such as:
- vision problems
- breathing difficulties
- learning problems
- walking difficulties

What causes preterm labour?

We do not know what causes most preterm labour. It is known that the chance of having preterm labour is more likely if you:
- have already had a preterm baby
- are carrying more than one baby (twins, triplets)
- smoke and are exposed to smoke in pregnancy
- do not eat a healthy diet
- are using alcohol and/or drugs
- work long hours which cause you to be very tired
- are physically or emotionally abused
- have a chronic illness, such as diabetes, heart disease, or kidney disease
- have a current bladder or kidney infection or high blood pressure

What can you and your partner do to decrease your risk of preterm labour?

- go to regular prenatal visits with your doctor or midwife
- follow *Canada's Food Guide to Healthy Eating*
- do not smoke, drink alcohol, or use drugs
- seek help if you are abused
- avoid strenuous work and do not work for more than 8 hours
- talk with your health care practitioner about extra stress in your life
- try to have time to rest each day
- wear your seat belt low and over the pelvic bones, with the shoulder belt worn normally
- listen to your body — talk with your health care practitioner if you feel that something is different

What are the signs of preterm labour?

- bleeding from the vagina
- a trickle or gush of fluid from your vagina
- stomach pains or bad cramps that don't go away
- lower back pain or pressure or a change in lower backache
- pressure in the pelvis, feeling that the baby is pushing down
- contractions — they feel regular and don't go away when you walk or rest
- an increase in the amount of vaginal discharge
- feeling that something is just not right

What do I do if I think I'm in preterm labour?

Contact your health care practitioner and go to the hospital right away. You need to be examined by a doctor or midwife. This can make a big difference to your baby's health.

Losing a Baby

A small number of parents lose their baby through a miscarriage, ectopic pregnancy, stillbirth, or other misfortune. These events bring emotions of grief, guilt, and despair, and can be difficult to handle. Each person grieves differently.

You may feel very sad and empty and have problems being around other pregnant women and mothers with babies. This is normal.

If your baby is stillborn, or dies near birth, you will have the opportunity to see and hold your baby. If you feel comfortable, take pictures of the baby alone or cuddled with you and your partner. Talk with your baby and say goodbye. Take your time. Don't let your baby go until you feel ready. Many women find this helps with their grieving, but this is your choice.

Mementos of your baby will be offered to you — things such as footprints, baby blanket, bracelets, or a lock of hair. You may not be able to look at them or you may think you don't want them, but this may change over time. You may wish to put them away for a while.

Knowing where to turn for help is important. Your health care practitioner can give you information, help you make difficult decisions and possibly set up counselling or referrals. Help is also available from the hospital social worker, chaplain, and nurses.

You will need physical and psychological postpartum care in hospital and in the community. In addition to emotional support, you may need help dealing with engorged breasts and a sore perineum. After you leave the hospital, your health care practitioner, the public health nurse, local crisis centre, and others who have been in a similar situation, can help.

The loss of a baby is difficult for both you and your partner. Being patient with each other helps. Men and women often react differently to losing a baby and time helps. Seek professional help.

Having a Baby after a Pregnancy Loss

If you have had a baby die in pregnancy and are now pregnant again, know that it is normal to be anxious. It is also normal to need to hear many times that your baby is doing well. Talk about your concerns with your health care practitioner. Also talk about your wishes for this birth. Some women may feel detached during the labour of a pregnancy following a stillbirth.

- Please do not drop in unannounced. Call first.

- Do not visit if you are sick.

- Wash your hands before touching the baby.

- Do not smoke in the house.

- If you have a cold sore, do not kiss the baby. Don't kiss anybody.

- Do not stay long.

- When you come, bring something, such as fresh bran muffins or a meal.

- Offer to help in whatever way you can.

Coming Home

What can we do to prepare for bringing the baby home?

- Bring your infant car seat to the hospital the day you go home. Learn how to use it correctly before your baby is born. The law requires that unless you come home in a taxi, you must have your baby in an infant seat that meets the Canadian Motor Vehicle Safety Standards. See page 131.

- Have diapers, blankets, clothes, and a safe, firm, sleeping space ready at home.

- Ask friends and family to help with older children and things such as preparing meals.

- Plan time for rest. Think of this as your "nesting time" when you can focus on each other and your new baby.

- Do not get a new pet when you are bringing your baby home.

What can your partner do to support you?

- arrange time off from work
- be present
- plan to share in the care for your baby
- plan to take responsibility for making meals and housework

What about visitors?

You may have a few visitors or dozens who want to visit. This can disturb your sleep and rest time. Let visitors know your visiting guidelines before your baby is born. That way, their visits can be a positive part of your recovery.

What about older brothers and sisters?

Brothers and sisters will react differently to the new baby. Some may love the baby and others may be angry. Many children will go back to acting like babies themselves for a while.

You can help prepare another child for the new baby by:

- Introducing the idea that families often have more than one child. Take your child to a playgroup. Make friends with parents who have children the same age.

- Making changes in routines several months before the baby arrives, or by making them well after. Some examples are toilet training or moving from a crib to a bed.

- Reading books or watching videos with your child about pregnancy and having a sibling.

- Giving your child a chance to practise staying with family or friends while you give birth. Do this sometime before the event.

How can we help an older child?

- If your child goes back to baby-like behaviours, wetting his pants, wanting the crib back, or wanting to breast or bottle feed, just relax. This will not last long.

- Give extra love and attention to your older child and tell her that you love her and the baby.

- Plan quiet feeding times with the new baby. Prepare a snack for your older child, listen to a favorite tape, or read together while you feed your baby.

- Give your child something to do to show that this is his baby too. He can tell stories or sing to the baby, or help to wash the baby. Mention how helpful he is.

- Make special time just for your older child each day.

- If you are still worried because nothing works with your older child, call your public health nurse or contact a local parent group.

Your Body After Pregnancy

Cramps

After birth, your uterus continues to contract. Cramps are most noticeable in the first few days. They may be more painful if you have had other children. Cramps are often felt most strongly while you breastfeed. They usually disappear after the first week. If they are severe, ask your health care practitioner about using something for pain.

Vaginal Discomfort and Care

The area between your legs (perineum) may be sore, bruised, and swollen. If you have stitches, you may feel more pain.

To ease discomfort:

- Cool the area with crushed ice or tap water for short-term relief. Do not put ice directly on your skin. Place a towel or pad between the ice and the skin.

- Clean your perineum by pouring warm water over your vaginal area or sitting in a warm bath.

- Use pain relievers as needed.

- Sit on a soft cushion to relieve pressure on your bottom.

- Continue to do Kegel (pelvic floor) exercises. See page 46.

Vaginal Bleeding (Lochia or Flow)

Following the baby's birth there will be bleeding and discharge from the vagina. This flow will usually last from two to six weeks. In the first two to three days, this flow is dark red with small clots about the size of a loonie. It should soak less than one maxi-pad in two hours and not smell bad. Flow then lessens and becomes brownish to pinkish in colour, similar to bleeding during the last days of a menstrual period. After the tenth day, the discharge is yellowish white or brown. If your flow does not become less or smells bad, call your health care practitioner.

Caution: use pads, not tampons, until any incision or vaginal tears are healed.

Menstruation (Period)

Your period may not start as long as your baby's only source of food is breastfeeding. If you do not breastfeed, your period will usually return four to nine weeks after the birth. You can become pregnant again before your period starts once more. If you do not want another pregnancy, use some form of birth control.

Urination (Peeing)

At first, it may be difficult to pee or tell when your bladder is full. It is helpful to pee at regular times to prevent the bladder from becoming too full. You may also find it hard to start peeing, or it may sting. To help, you can pour warm water over your perineum or pee in the shower or bath.

You may have some leakage of urine for up to three months and sometimes longer after your baby is born. This is called urinary incontinence. A cough, sneeze, laugh, or physical activity can make this happen. Doing Kegel exercises can help to control urine leakage. For most women, this gradually goes away.

Bowel Movements

After birth, your bowels are often sluggish. This is due to stretched muscles, a sore perineum, and some pain medications. Most mothers have a bowel movement within two to three days after birth.

To make bowel movements easier:
- drink plenty of fluids, especially water
- eat foods such as whole grains, bran, dried fruits (especially prunes and figs), fresh fruits, vegetables, and juices
- if the first suggestions do not work, try using stool softeners that can be bought at drug stores

If you have stitches, you may find that supporting the area with a cool, clean, wet pad is comforting when you have your first bowel movement.

Hemorrhoids

Hemorrhoids are painful, itchy and sometimes bleeding veins that bulge out around your anus. Hemorrhoids can develop in pregnancy or from the pushing and straining of birth. They often go away in a few weeks after birth.

To help hemorrhoids:
- try not to stand for long periods
- lie down to take pressure off your bottom
- keep bowel movements soft to avoid straining when going to the bathroom
- sit or soak in a warm bath to bring relief

Weight Changes

- It took nine months to become the size and shape you are. It will take a few months to return to your pre-pregnancy weight.

- Do not diet. Focus on nutritious eating and getting 20 minutes of light exercise a day.

- Breastfeeding will help you lose weight. It is especially helpful along with healthy eating and regular activity, such as walking. Many women find that most weight loss happens in the second six months of breastfeeding.

- Start exercising slowly.

Call your health care practitioner if:

- Your flow gets heavier rather than lighter.

- Your flow has a foul smell.

- You have flu-like symptoms or an unexplained fever over 38°C.

- The stitches on your perineum open up, drain, or become infected.

- You have pain, swelling, and redness near your caesarean incision.

- The stitches on your caesarean incision open up, drain, or become infected.

- You have redness or pain in the calf of your leg.

- You have a tender, reddened area on your breast that is not relieved by more frequent breastfeeding.

- You have to pee often and it hurts when you pee.

- You have constipation that is not relieved with diet, lots of fluids, exercise, and stool softeners.

Life With Your Baby

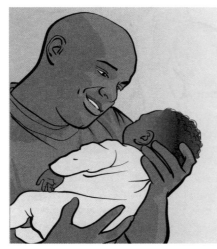

Having a baby is a special time in your life. It is a time of changes — both physical and emotional. During your pregnancy, your body changes, your hormones are changing, and you have to come to terms with the joys and the care of the baby growing inside you. After the birth you will have to deal with your own changes and take care of your baby's needs too.

While having a baby is usually a time of celebration, families and the people around you may forget that this can be a stressful time. They forget that you may find it hard to cope with all the sudden changes and stresses in your life.

In the first few days after birth, up to 80% of mothers feel distress. This is commonly called the *baby blues*. You may feel restless, irritable, tearful, tired, discouraged, sad, or helpless. You may swing between a feeling of sadness and a sense of happiness. You may suddenly feel full of energy and want to talk a lot. These mood changes can be due to many things, such as the quick drop of your hormone levels after birth or the pain and tiredness from your labour and birth. They can also be the result of looking after your baby for 24 hours a day and not getting enough sleep. Most of the time the blues do not last very long. They will go away on their own in one or two weeks.

A small number of women will go on to have what is called postpartum depression. Talk to you health care practitioner or public health nurse if:

- the baby blues do not go away within two weeks
- you feel unable to cope
- you are concerned about taking care of yourself or your baby

You can also call the BC NurseLine, at 1-866-215-4700, to speak confidentially with a registered nurse. There is someone there to answer your call 24 hours a day, seven days a week. Or, you can visit the Pacific Post Partum Society's website at www.postpartum.org/index2.html for helpful information and advice.

Taking Care of Yourself

Remember there are two people who need to be taken care of — your baby and you. Your blues may turn into something more serious.

Each day ask yourself, have I:

- Eaten at least three meals today and also had healthy snacks in between if hungry?

- Had some exercise, such as walking with my baby in a stroller?

- Taken a short break? Done something that is nice to do? When your baby is asleep or your partner can take over, take a nap, read a book, take a bath, or sit in the garden.

- Talked with friends or family about my feelings?

- Met with a support group of people who understand my feelings? Your public health office can tell you about postpartum support groups.

- Shared the responsibilities of taking care of our baby with my partner? Make a plan with your partner so you can share the care of your baby.

One of the best lessons I learned in taking care of my baby was the importance of sleep (hers and mine). I tried to nap the minute she did, because I could never count on her sleeping for very long. Since I needed to be well rested to deal with her colic, the housework had to wait!

What can partners and others do to help the mother?

- Ask the mother to talk to you about her feelings. Listen and try to understand. Don't worry that you can't solve her problems.

- Be there for her and tell her that you love her. Praise her for something she's done.

- Share the responsibility of caring for the baby and the household.

- Make sure she has some time to herself away from the house. She can do things like going for a walk or a drive or having quiet time by herself.

- Accept help from family and friends.

- Be affectionate but wait until she expresses desire before encouraging sex.

- Contact a postpartum support group.

- Get help from your health care practitioners and let them help you both.

Postpartum Depression

Fifteen percent of women who have a new baby have depression that sets in after the birth. It is called *postpartum depression*. It is not possible to know who will get postpartum depression, but some risk factors are:

- having had a previous postpartum depression
- having a history of depression, including anxiety and panic attacks
- having a family history of postpartum depression
- having lack of support

Other factors that can contribute to postpartum depression are:

- being a young mother
- having an unexpected pregnancy, or feeling unsure about your pregnancy
- not having enough money or feeling isolated from other people
- an unstable marriage
- difficult life events, such as the death of a loved one or loss of a job
- violence or abuse
- chronic or serious health problems
- having a baby with health problems
- having a baby that you feel has a demanding nature
- having a baby is not what you thought it would be

How can I tell if I might have postpartum depression?

You can tell if you:

- have a depressed mood
- have a loss of interest or pleasure in day-to-day activities
- are sleeping too little or too much
- are physically overactive or have no energy
- swing from hunger to loss of appetite
- feel very tired
- feel mostly sad, unhappy, irritable, or guilty, and have lots of crying spells
- feel you are worthless
- have a hard time concentrating
- have thoughts of death or killing yourself that keep coming back

Do these factors or feelings relate to you? If they do, talk with your health care practitioner, partner, or supportive friends.

What can be done?

Postpartum depression can have many negative effects on you and your family. It is treatable. Talking about your feelings with your partner or a friend may help for a short time. If your symptoms last longer than a few days, get help.

If you are thinking of hurting yourself, your baby, or others, contact your health care practitioner right away. Do not try to deal with depression by yourself. There are people who help women in this situation. Remember — this is common and can be treated.

Being a Supportive Partner

Today partners are taking an active role, not only in child care but during pregnancy as well. No matter where you are starting from, you are not alone. Whatever you are feeling — fear, excitement or panic — other people have felt the same thing. Examine your feelings. Parenthood is a new and exciting state in your life. Here are a few feelings new fathers have reported.

- My partner is so involved with the baby that there is no time for us.

- I don't have friends who are parents. None of my old friends understand what I'm going through.

- I'm scared of the baby. What if I drop her? My partner is much more at ease with changing, bathing, handling, and playing with our baby than I am.

- How will I be able to protect and provide for my new family?

- I used to feel immortal. Now I have to be here to look after my family. I had never thought about life insurance before.

- I'm afraid of being replaced by the baby. My partner loves the baby so much and only seems to let me be involved when she says it's OK.

- This is a whole new role for me. I'm not sure I like having to do more chores around the house. I want my partner and my old life back.

- I'm so tired. Getting a whole night's sleep is all I want right now.

- How can someone like me be a good Dad? I don't know what I'm doing.

Here are some things you can do:
- Talk with your partner as often as possible about your feelings, what you need, and how you can best be involved in caring for your baby.

- Support your partner while she is breastfeeding. Bring her a glass of water, milk, or juice.

- Don't worry about being scared of the baby. You are not alone with this feeling. Always think safety first. Ask yourself what is the safest thing to do here? By handling your baby, you will become more comfortable. You probably didn't feel comfortable the first time you drove a car either.

- Lay your baby on your chest and relax together. Children need closeness with both parents.

- Change your baby's diaper, give him a bath, dress, sing, dance, or just cuddle your baby. Always wash your hands first.

- Play with your baby as often as possible. It's OK to choose toys you like to play with too.

- Remember not to leave your baby alone even for a second on a change table, counter, chair, or couch, or in the bath.

- Don't leave your baby alone with your pet.

- Get enough sleep, exercise, go for walks as a family, and eat healthy foods.

- Listen to other parents. They have been through this.

- Get involved with other dads — from your prenatal classes, work, or from a new parenting class.

- Remember — all parents make mistakes.

- Enjoy each phase of being a parent. It won't come around again with this child.

- Plan to have time for activities other than parenting. Do tag team parenting — let one parent be "off" sometimes.

- Talk with your partner about the best method of birth control for both of you.

- Don't expect your partner to be her old self in a week or two — recovery from birth takes time.

Parenting Can Be Frustrating

Bringing home a baby is not easy. Your family has changed, your schedule will change, and you will be more tired than you have ever been in your life. This is normal!

We were both getting frustrated being in the house so much. The baby would cry at times and I'd think, "What have we done? I want my old life back." But then the good times are so great, I can't imagine not being a dad. It does all work out in the end but the first few months were tough. If I could give advice it would be to take help when it's offered and know when to just walk away for a few minutes.

Here are a few frustrations mothers have expressed:
- I don't feel as though I have the same body I had before pregnancy.

- I have never been so tired in my life.

- I get so frustrated when the baby cries and I can't soothe her, and the crying seems endless.

- I can't do the same activities I did before having the baby.

- I was so tired, and there I was acting like a happy hostess to all these visitors who wanted to see the baby.

- Everyone has an opinion on how we should take care of our baby.

A few frustrations partners have expressed:
- I didn't seem to have any time for myself. I was either working or taking care of the baby.

- I couldn't seem to find a way to comfort him that would make him stop crying.

- I have never been so sleep starved in my life. I just wanted one complete night's rest.

- It seemed like we never left the house.

- I really miss having sex and my partner isn't as close as she used to be.

Hints on staying calm:
- Anytime I started to lose my temper I put the baby down somewhere safe and left the room.

- I realized how much I needed my sleep. I got my family to help by taking the baby out for a walk every day so I had time to nap and catch up.

- I'd plan a nap for the late afternoon. That gave me more strength to handle my baby's nighttime needs.

- I talked to my partner about what the baby and I might need. He used to wait until I told him what to do. Now he just does what needs to be done.

- We would talk about how we felt. We became very good at being frank about our needs.

- We would plan to spend time together, just the two of us, at least once a week. Even if it was to just go for a walk. We would ask a friend or family member to help out by watching the baby.

- We found it really helped to talk to a group of new parents. We got together with our prenatal group to swap stories and advice. It was reassuring to find out that most of them felt the same way we did.

- When we found things were getting too difficult with the baby, we talked with the public health nurse. She told us about a parenting group that was really helpful.

Being a Single Parent

Being a single parent is common today. For some people, family and friends are a good source of support. Others may not have family and friends close by. If you don't have a partner, that does not mean you will be alone. There are people and programs to help you, and it is important to find them. To find these programs, contact your public health nurse or social worker, or talk with your health care practitioner.

Some of the places where parents meet are:
- parents and infant groups at the public health office
- pregnancy outreach programs
- breastfeeding groups
- movie theatres for parents and babies
- local playgrounds
- community centres
- family resource centres
- spiritual or religious groups

Doing the Paperwork

Leave from Work

Two different kinds of leave from work are available for parents: *maternity leave* and *parental leave.*

- Maternity leave is available only to the birth mother. If she's been employed prior to the birth, she may qualify for Employment Insurance benefits during this time.

- Parental leave is available to the birth mother and/or father. If they have been employed prior to the birth, they may qualify for Employment Insurance benefits during this time. The birth mother usually takes parental leave right after her pregnancy leave is over. Adoptive parents also qualify for parental leave.

Under the British Columbia *Employment Standards Act,* employees are entitled to a leave of absence from work, without pay, so they can spend time with a new child. A birth mother is entitled to up to 17 consecutive weeks of unpaid *maternity leave.* This leave period may be extended by up to six consecutive weeks if an employee is unable to return to work for reasons related to the birth. An employer may require an employee to provide a doctor's certificate in support of a request for leave or a leave extension. The Act also provides for *parental leave* of 35 weeks for birth mothers and 37 weeks for fathers and adopting parents.

Please note: This is for general information only. It is not a legal document. Please refer to the *Employment Standards Act and Regulation* for purposes of interpretation and application of the law.

Changing Your Will

If either or both of you die, you want to be sure your child is well taken care by someone you trust. Decide who will be the best guardian to look after your child, then ask if they will do it. After you get their consent, you can either make a will or change your current will.

Registering the Birth

The birth registration creates a legal record of your baby's birth and legal name. As soon as possible after the birth of your baby (within 30 days), you must fill out the *Registration of Live Birth* form. Send this form to any Vital Statistics office or Government Agent's office. There is no cost if you do this within 30 days of your baby's birth. Normally, both parents sign the registration form. If the father does not sign it, none of his personal information can be registered or printed on the baby's birth certificate.

The *Registration of Live Birth* form is available from:
- the hospital where you give birth
- your midwife, if you give birth at home
- any Vital Statistics office
- the government website: www.vs.gov.bc.ca/forms

If you need help filling out your form, contact your local Vital Statistics Office. The number can be found in the blue pages of your local phone book.

Getting a Birth Certificate
A birth certificate is used for official identification and as proof of a person's legal name, date, and place of birth. It is an important document to have. To get a birth certificate, you can fill out the order form on the back of the Registration of Live Birth form. Another option is to fill out an Application for Service form from the Vital Statistics Agency. You can also print a form from the government website listed in Resources at the back of the book. There is a fee for a birth certificate.

Points to Remember

Call the Employment Standards information line for more information on any provincial rules. Look in the blue pages of your phone book for the phone number. You can also visit the Employment Standards Branch website, www.labour.gov.bc.ca/esb, where you'll find links to a number of fact sheets. One of these deals with leaves.

For information on federal rules and Employment Insurance for maternity, parental or other leaves, call Human Resources Development Canada. Check the blue pages of your phone book for the Government of Canada section and look under "Employment." You can also visit their website at: www.hrdc.gc.ca/en/ei/types/special.shtml.

- Talk to your employer about any other benefits your place of work may have.

- Your employer must keep your job or a similar position while you are on maternity or parental leave.

- Your benefits, such as medical coverage, will continue during your unpaid leave if you keep paying your share of the premium cost.

Choosing a Name

Yes, you can choose any name you like for your baby. Your baby must have a first name (given name) and a last name (surname). You can give your baby one or more middle names if you wish. The baby's surname can be different from the mother or father's surname. The baby's surname can be two surnames, hyphenated or combined together.

Arranging for Tax Benefits

After your baby's birth, you can apply for the following two benefits, and register your child for the Goods Services Tax/Harmonized Sales Tax (GST/HST) credit, using a single application form:

- The Canada Child Tax Benefit. (This includes both the Child Tax Benefit and the National Child Benefit Supplement.)

- BC Family Benefits. (This includes both the Family Bonus and Earned Income Benefit.)

The form to complete is called the *Canada Child Tax Benefit* application. It is a separate form from the *Registration of Live Birth*. It is often available at the hospital or from your midwife. If you do not receive this form, call Canada Child Tax Benefit (toll-free: 1-800-387-1193) or look under "Child and Family Benefits" in the blue pages of your telephone book. You can also visit www.cra.gc.ca online.

Arranging for Medical Coverage

To get medical coverage, you must fill out the *Medical Services Plan (MSP) Baby Registration* form. This form should be filled out and sent within 60 days of your baby's birth. It is available at the hospital or from your midwife.

If you pay your own premiums, or if the premiums are paid by Health Canada, send the form to the MSP address on the form. If your premiums are to be paid by the Ministry of Human Resources, take the form to your social worker. If premiums are paid through your place of work or union welfare plan, take the form to your group administration for authorization.

A British Columbia CareCard for your baby will be sent to you six to eight weeks after the MSP office receives the completed form. In the first 60 days after birth, your baby will get medical care using your medical number.

Arranging for Drug Coverage

Fair PharmaCare Coverage gives financial help with prescription drugs costs. To register for Fair PharmaCare financial help you must have:

- lived in British Columbia for at least three months
- medical services coverage with the Medical Services Plan of British Columbia
- sent in an income tax return for the right taxation year

If you are already registered, your baby will automatically be registered. If you need information or wish to register, phone the PharmaCare Program. Look in the Provincial section of the phone book blue pages or visit the website at https://pharmacare.moh.hnet.bc.ca.

PharmaCare offers a voluntary Monthly Deductible Payment Option. This is for families with annual incomes over $15,000 who do not have third party insurance benefits through work. It is to help people who think they will have high drug costs. For more information, contact the Fair PharmaCare Registration toll-free at 1-800-387-4977.

Next Steps

Babysitters

You may decide to leave your baby with family or friends for short periods of time in the first months after your baby is born. You should know and feel comfortable with the person you choose to leave your baby with — even if it's just for a few minutes. Check to see if the sitter has taken a recognized babysitter course.

- Have her hold and play with your baby and watch how they act together.

- Ask her how she would deal with a crying/fussy baby.

- Watch as she feeds and diapers your baby.

Be clear about your expectations regarding care of your baby. Things you might mention:
- never leave your baby unattended on a change table, couch, or sofa
- how often you expect your baby to be checked when sleeping
- it is never OK to hit or shake your baby

Pay attention to how you feel about the potential babysitter. Do you feel secure and confident? Or tense, worried, and ill at ease? Remember — the goal of leaving your baby with a sitter is for you to have time to relax.

When the babysitter arrives:
- Allow time for her to play with your baby (if awake) before you leave.

- Stress that the baby be placed on his back for sleeping.

- Review with her your expectations regarding care and attention to your baby. See above.

- Show your babysitter where things are kept.

- Reinforce that to warm breast milk or formula, the bottle should be set in a container of warm tap water. Milk for your baby should never be warmed on the stove or in a microwave. A microwave will heat the breast milk (or formula) unevenly and can burn your baby's mouth.

To make the babysitter's job easier, and to make you feel more confident about leaving your baby, be sure to leave this information:
- Where you are going, when you expect to return, and how you can be reached.

- Insist that if there are any problems, she should call you home early. Remind her she must never shake or hit your baby.

- Keep these emergency telephone numbers close to the phone:
  - fire
  - police
  - poison information
  - doctor
  - hospital (pediatric emergency number)
  - helpful neighbour (name and number)
  - closest relative
  - taxi

- Some personal information may be needed in an emergency, so leave the following close to the phone as well:
  - baby's and your last name(s)
  - home phone number
  - home address

What should we ask ourselves when choosing birth control methods?

- How effective is it?

- Will the method affect breastfeeding?

- How easy is it to use?

- How much does it cost?

- How do we feel about the method?

- Will we be protected against STIs?

Need more information? Talk with your health care practitioner or call the Options for Sexual Health Facts of Life Line, the BC NurseLine, or see the *BC HealthGuide* handbook. See the Resources section at the back of the book for contact information.

Family Planning

Once your pregnancy is over and you have given birth to your baby, you and your partner will have to think about birth control methods. As soon as you start having sex, it is possible to get pregnant.

Which methods of birth control are NOT effective?
- withdrawing the penis before ejaculation
- douching or rinsing the vagina with a water-based solution after intercourse

Is breastfeeding an effective birth control method?
Although there are no absolute guarantees, breastfeeding may be effective birth control if:
- your baby is under six months
- your baby is exclusively breastfed, day and night
- your baby is not given a bottle or soother
- you have not started your period

However, as soon as your baby is sleeping longer at night or having other foods or fluids, breastfeeding is less likely to work as a birth control method.

Single Use Birth Control Methods

Type	Advantages	Disadvantages
Male Condom (85–98% effective) A latex sheath rolled onto the erect penis before any contact with the vagina, carefully taken off the penis after ejaculation to prevent spillage, and then discarded. It is recommended to use with water-based lubrication.	• does not require a prescription • protects against most STIs • safe while breastfeeding	• condoms can fail by falling off or breaking • some men and women are allergic to the latex and/or the lubricant
Female Condom (79–95% effective) A polyurethane sheath inserted to cover the wall of the vagina during intercourse. May need to use water-based lubricant.	• protects against most STIs • safe while breastfeeding	• can be difficult to insert • can be noisy during sex • can be expensive
Diaphragm (82–94%) effective **Cervical Cap (80–90% effective)** Rubber cup-like barriers inserted into the vagina to cover the entrance to the uterus. Must be fitted by a doctor. They must be used with a spermicide and left in at least 6 to 8 hours after intercourse. Need to carefully clean with soap and warm water when removed, and inspected for holes. The woman must learn how to insert them correctly.	• has long life with proper care • can be inserted up to 6 hours before intercourse • safe while breastfeeding	• some women find it difficult to insert properly, which causes them to fail • some risk of allergic reactions to rubber or spermicide • more risk of bladder infections • cannot be used during menstruation • must be refitted after pregnancy or weight changes

Type	Advantages	Disadvantages
Spermicides (71–85% effective) Creams, gels, or foams that destroy sperm. These must be inserted high into the vagina 15 to 20 minutes before intercourse. They only work for about one hour.	• does not require a prescription • adds extra lubrication • use as a backup to other methods • safe while breastfeeding	• can create sensitivity or allergic reactions • no protection from STIs (can actually increase risk)
Contraceptive sponges (72–95% effective) A sponge treated with spermicide that is placed over the cervix. Sometimes used with a condom, diaphragm, or cervical cap. Must be left in place for 6 to 8 hours and works for 24 hours.	• does not require a prescription • use as backup to other methods • safe while breastfeeding	• can create sensitivity or allergic reactions • no protection from STIs

Long-term Birth Control Methods

Type	Advantages	Disadvantages
Intra-uterine Contraception Device (IUD) (98–99% effective) A small, flexible piece of plastic (with copper wire or progestin) inserted into the uterus by a doctor. A small string hangs through the cervix allowing the woman to check that it is in position. Most suitable for women who have had a child.	• can be left in place for 2 1/2 to 5 years • removed whenever necessary • progestin IUDs may make periods lighter • safe while breastfeeding	• may cause more painful or heavier periods • no protection from STIs • may cause increased risk of pelvic inflammatory disease if an STI is contracted
Oral Contraceptive Pills (92–99% effective) The "pill" is usually a combination of the hormones estrogen and progestin, and prevents ovulation. Pills are prescribed by doctors and must be taken on a regular daily schedule.	• easy to use • may regulate periods • may lower the risk of some types of cancers (ovarian, endometrial, etc.)	• may have estrogen-related side effects (minor weight gain, headaches, etc.) • women who smoke should not take the pill as it increases the risk of heart disease • women with some medical conditions may not be able to use the pill • taking antibiotics may interfere with the pill's effectiveness • no protection from STIs • may lower breast milk supply and should be used with caution if breastfeeding is not well established

Type	Advantages	Disadvantages
Transdermal Patch (97 – 99% effective) The patch works the same way as the birth control pill but is worn on the skin and replaced once a week.	• easy to use • may regulate periods	• about 5% of patches become unstuck, but may remain effective if replaced within 24 hours • need to check every day that it's on • some women may have side effects • no protection from STIs • not recommended for women who are breastfeeding
Depo-Provera (97 – 99% effective) A hormonal contraception given as an injection by a doctor every 11 to 13 weeks. It prevents ovulation.	• easy to use • may cause lighter periods or may stop them • no estrogen-related side effects • not affected by antibiotic use	• some side effects (irregular periods, depression, weight gains, etc.) • return to fertility may take 1 – 2 years • no protection from STIs • may lower breast milk supply • mothers must have more calcium and vitamin D while on Depo-Provera The use of Depo-Provera is linked with the loss of bone mineral density. This could lead to osteoporosis and related bone fractures in later life. A review of a woman's risks and benefits of using this method of birth control need to be discussed with a health care practitioner.

Permanent Birth Control Methods

Type	Advantages	Disadvantages
Sterilization: Vasectomy (male) **Tubal Occlusion (female) (99.9% effective)** The tubes carrying sperm from the testes in men or the eggs from the ovaries in women are surgically cut or plugged. Males must have follow-up visits to determine when sperm production has ceased. Both can be done on an outpatient basis. Tubal occlusion can be done during a caesarean birth.	• no fears of pregnancy • both covered by the BC Medical Services Plan • safe while breastfeeding	• slight chance of complications from surgery • permanent; reversals rarely work • no protection from STIs
Fertility Awareness Techniques (80% effective) Involves accurately predicting the menstrual cycle to determine when a woman is fertile and when sex should be avoided or other protection used. Special training from a qualified fertility counsellor is needed to use this method effectively.	• inexpensive • teaches about fertility patterns • safe while breastfeeding	• the woman must have a regular cycle • may not work during breastfeeding as menses is changing • requires careful monitoring of the woman's cycle and avoiding sex or using extra protection • no protection from STIs

Emergency Birth Control

Emergency Contraceptive Pill **(74–99% effective if taken within** **72 hours of unprotected sex)** Used as an emergency option after unprotected sex or after a failed birth control method. Most effective if taken as soon as possible, but may work up to 120 hours after intercourse. Prescribed by a doctor or may be issued by a pharmacist and at some public health offices.	• provides a second chance to prevent an unplanned pregnancy in case another method fails • a single dose of the pill will not likely affect breastfeeding	• may cause nausea and vomiting • may disrupt your period • no protection from STIs

Notes

Your Baby

This section of the book will help you learn about your baby. It gives you lots of information on how your baby grows, how to breastfeed, and helpful hints on caring for your baby. You may have received this book after your baby was born. Maybe you got it when your adoptive baby joined your family. Be assured that if any of the things recommended earlier in the book did not happen, you can still make a difference. Your baby's brain and body growth happen in the womb, but the growth (especially of the brain) continues in the first two or more years. You as a parent and your family can make an important difference in your baby's development.

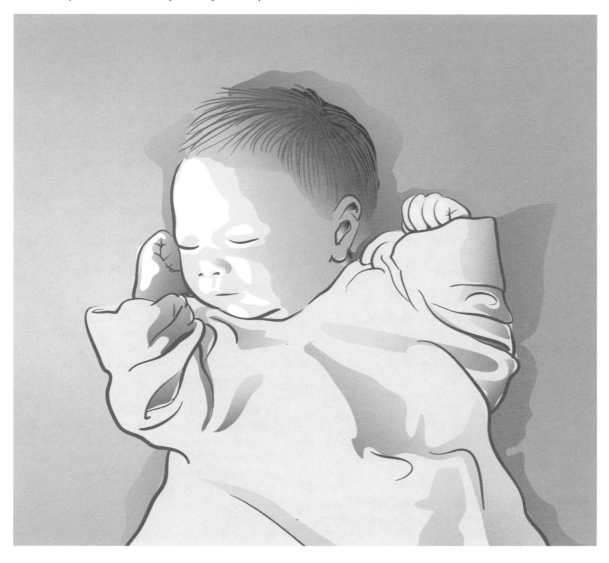

Breastfeeding Your Baby

Breastfeeding is the normal way to feed your baby. Breast milk provides all the nutrition your baby needs. It has hundreds of antibodies, enzymes, and other factors that will protect your baby from infections and disease. Breast milk is always at the right temperature, easy to provide, always handy, changes as your baby grows, and is free. Babies who are breastfed have better mental development and emotional security. They score higher on developmental and cognitive (IQ) tests. They also have better jaw and tooth development and improved immune systems.

Why is it important to breastfeed my baby?
Babies who are breastfed have lower rates of:
- Sudden Infant Death Syndrome (SIDS)
- obesity
- Type I diabetes
- childhood cancers, including leukemia and lymphoma
- pneumonia and other respiratory infections
- coughs and colds
- gastrointestinal infections
- vomiting, diarrhea, constipation
- urinary tract infections
- ear infections that can damage hearing
- meningitis
- Crohn's disease, ulcerative colitis
- Celiac disease
- asthma, allergies, and eczema
- heart disease and liver disease in adulthood

What are the benefits for the mother?
- a faster return to pre-pregnancy weight
- stronger bones in later life
- lower rates of breast and ovarian cancer

How can we get a good start?
- It is important to put your baby on your bare chest, especially in the first few days after birth. This is called *skin-to-skin.*

- Offer your breast soon after birth. Most babies will show readiness to feed in the first 30 to 60 minutes after birth.

- Feed your baby frequently — 8 or more times a day.

- After your baby's first breastfeeding, she may sleep for a few hours so may not feed 8 times.

- In their second 24 hours, babies wake up a lot to feed — 8 or more times a day and, in the beginning, very often during the night.

- Look for signs that your baby is ready to nurse. These are called *feeding cues.* Feeding cues include bringing her hands to her mouth, rooting (moves her head as if she is looking for your nipple), or being restless. Crying is a late cue — this means you have not noticed the other feeding cues.

- In the first three to four days after birth, your baby may lose some weight. This is normal.

- Give your baby only your breast milk. The small amount of colostrum (first milk) your baby gets in the first two to three days is perfect until the amount of your milk increases.

- You can hand express drops of colostrum to give your baby.

- Be sure you are in a comfortable position to nurse and get your baby on your breast well — a good latch.

- Have someone stay with you — in hospital and at home — to help.

- Make yourself comfortable whenever you are breastfeeding. Have your back, feet, and arms well supported. Use a footstool and put a pillow on your lap and/or under your arm for support. Holding your baby up during the feeding will be uncomfortable and tiring to your arms.

- Support your breast with your free hand. You can usually let go of the breast once your baby is latched on and sucking.

- Call your public health nurse or the BC NurseLine, at 1-866-215-4700, if you need extra support to keep going or if you have questions. It's worth it, for you and your baby.

Comfortable Positions

The position you use isn't important as long as both you and your baby are comfortable, relaxed, and your baby is able to latch onto the breast. You may find that the modified cradle or football hold is easiest to use until you and your baby learn how to latch on well.

Modified cradle position

Football hold

Side-lying

Cradle position

Latching On

Correctly latching your baby onto the breast is an important step in successful breastfeeding. A poor latch may cause sore nipples, a hungry baby, and a smaller milk supply. If you feel pain when your baby is on the breast (not a passing discomfort) a poor latch may be the problem. Gently remove your baby from the breast and start again. To take your baby off your breast and break the suction from her sucking, gently place a finger in the corner of your baby's mouth.

How can I get a good latch?

- Unwrap your baby. Blankets make it hard for baby to be close enough to latch well.

- Turn your baby's whole body to face you (tummy to tummy).

- Support your breast but keep your fingers well back from the areola (brown part).

- Aim your nipple high in your baby's mouth.

- Touch the baby's lips with your breast to help her to open her mouth wide.

- Wait until your baby opens her mouth wide, like a yawn.

- Bring your baby in close to you.

- Put your hand on her shoulders, not her head.

When is my baby well latched?

- The initial latch may hurt but you shouldn't feel pain in the nipple area. You may feel a tug.

- Your baby's chin is touching your breast and her nose is slightly away from the breast.

- Your baby begins to suck. Her cheeks will be full and rounded. If there are dimples in the cheeks, the baby may not be latched well.

Baby is well latched onto the breast.

- While sucking, your baby may suck quickly, then more slowly, with short rest pauses. You may be able to hear the baby swallowing. Listen for a "ca" sound. You will hear this more easily when your milk increases.

- Sometimes you may hear your baby gulping, especially if you have lots of milk.

- Clicking or smacking sounds may mean that your baby is not latched correctly.

- Your nipple looks rounded, not flattened, when your baby comes off your breast.

- The nipple does not have any cracks, blisters, or bleeding.

- You can't easily slide her off the breast.

The Let-down Reflex

Let-down happens as milk is released into milk ducts in your breast. This usually happens when your baby sucks on your breast. You may even have a let-down when your baby or someone else's baby cries, or for no reason at all. Some women don't feel the let-down. Others may feel a pins and needles or tingling sensation. Others will have a very strong sensation or discomfort. Other signs of let-down include leaking milk from the opposite breast, cramping, increased vaginal flow, increased thirst, and relaxation.

Can I have a let-down if I'm not feeding my baby?

Yes. If you find you are soaking your shirts with milk at inconvenient times:

- Wear one or more breast pads as needed. Change these pads to keep the skin dry.

- Wear dark patterned clothes to hide the milk spilled on your tops.

- Cross your arms and press the palm of your hand on the nipple area when you feel the let-down happening. This will help to hold back the milk.

What if my let-down is slow?

Make sure you are comfortable when breastfeeding. If you are embarrassed or anxious about breastfeeding, it may take a little longer for the milk to flow well.

- Find a private, quiet place if you are uncomfortable.

- Sit or lie comfortably.

- Have a drink handy (non-alcoholic).

- Massage your breasts or apply a warm face cloth to the breast before feeding.

If you have followed these tips and still have a problem with let-down, talk with your public health nurse, midwife, or a lactation consultant — a person with extra knowledge to help breastfeeding mothers and babies.

How Much and How Long?

How often and how long should I feed my baby?

- In the early days, breastfeed from both breasts to help make your milk supply. Later your baby may still feed from both breasts, or may be satisfied after one.

- Feed on the first breast until the baby falls away from your breast. This usually tells you that your baby has had enough milk. Don't rush though — your baby may be just resting and not yet finished.

- Your breast should feel soft. It's important to empty the breast well.

- After burping, offer the other breast.

- Let your baby be your guide.

- If still hungry, your baby will latch on, suck, and swallow.

- Begin the next feeding on the breast you didn't use at the last feeding, or the one you finished last.

- Some babies feed very often at first — as much as every one to two hours, from the start of one feed to the start of the next — and then go for longer periods between feedings. This cluster feeding is normal.

- It is normal to feed eight or more times in 24 hours.

- There is no set amount of time for how long your baby should feed at your breast. In the early days it may seem as though it takes a very long time to feed your baby.

- Ask for help if you are having difficulty or feedings take longer than an hour. Call your public health nurse, midwife, or community or hospital breastfeeding clinic.

- After your milk supply is well established, the feedings will be shorter.

She Said

After reading all about the benefits of breastfeeding I was excited to get started. But after a couple days of nursing I started to get discouraged. The process of engorgement left my breasts swollen and very sore, not to mention the pain in my nipples. I felt like giving up. However, after a couple of weeks it got much easier and I actually began to enjoy the special time spent with my baby. The discomfort and short-term pain were long forgotten, as I knew I was doing the best for my baby.

Points to Remember

From 2 weeks to about 3 months, babies should gain about 180 – 240 grams (6 – 8 ounces) per week.

From about 3 to 6 months, babies should gain about 90 – 180 grams (3 – 6 ounces) per week.

We both felt that breastfeeding would be the best thing to do for our baby. I got involved by bringing my wife a glass of water every time she sat down to nurse the baby. We ate well, exercised, didn't drink and generally were the most healthy we've ever been during those two years. She would express milk sometimes so she could go out for a break and I would take over and do the feeding. I really liked the closeness at those times.

Points to Remember

Your baby needs to nurse often. Even though she only drinks 10 to 100 ml (1 tablespoon to 1/2 cup) per day in the first few days, nursing will help increase the milk supply for your baby as she needs it.

How can I tell that my baby is getting enough milk in the first weeks?

- Your baby is feeding eight or more times a day after the first 24 hours.

- You see your baby sucking and swallowing. You will hear a "ca" sound during the feeding.

- In the first three days of life, your baby has 1 to 2 wet diapers per day. By days four to six, as your milk supply increases, your baby should have 5 or more wet diapers a day. His urine should be pale yellow.

- Your baby has 2 to 3 or more bowel movements a day. After the first four to six weeks it is common for bowel movements to be less often. They may come once every few days. As long as the bowel movement is loose and the baby has wet diapers, this is normal.

- Your baby is satisfied and content after most feedings.

- Your baby has returned to his birth weight by about two weeks.

- Your breasts are full before the feedings and softer after. After several weeks, it is normal to have soft breasts all the time and still have lots of milk.

Call your health care practitioner, the BC NurseLine, or Dial-A-Dietitian right away if your baby:
- does not have 1–2 wet diapers in the first 3 days
- does not have 5 very wet diapers each day after 4–6 days of age
- does not have at least 2–3 bowel movements a day after 4 days of age
- is not interested in feeding and often goes without feeding for 4–5 hours in the first few week

See the Resources section for contact numbers.

Baby's Age	Baby's Stomach Size	Amount Baby May Drink in 24 hours
1–2 days	Size of a cooked chick pea or a hazelnut	10 to 100 ml or 1 tablespoon to 1/2 cup
3–7 days	Size of a cherry or a teaspoon	200 ml or almost 1 cup
2–5 weeks	Size of a walnut or a tablespoon	700 to 800 ml or about 21/2 to 31/2 cups

If you are worried that your baby isn't getting enough milk, remember that the size of your baby's stomach is very small. (Adapted with permission by the Best Start Resource Centre.)

Is it OK to use a soother?

Soothers should not be given in the first six to eight weeks when a baby is learning to breastfeed. You should not use a soother if your baby has any problems with feeding or you have low milk production. If your baby uses a soother, he may feed less often at the breast, which will decrease milk production. Full term babies should not be given soothers. If you choose to use a soother, wait until breastfeeding is well established.

Breastfeeding babies rarely need soothers as their need to suck for comfort, stress release, and pleasure can easily be met by breastfeeding. A soother is one way to comfort a baby but other choices include breastfeeding, holding your baby, or letting her suck on your finger. Many people think soother use prevents thumb sucking. This is not true. Babies normally suck on their fingers and thumbs. If you choose to use a soother, also remember to hold your baby a lot.

What about spitting up?

Spitting up small amounts after a meal is very common in the first few months of life and is not the same as vomiting. Spitting up usually stops as your baby grows. Spitting up is not a concern as long as your baby is healthy, happy, and gaining weight well.

What about hiccups?

Many babies have frequent hiccups, which can be quite loud. Baby's hiccups often bother the parents more than they seem to bother the baby. Hiccups go away by themselves.

How do I burp my baby?

Burping between feedings may help bring up air bubbles and prevent some spitting up. To burp your baby, gently rub or pat her on the back. Thumping your baby on the back can make her spit up all the milk that was just taken. Sometimes just sitting your baby upright works.

When your baby has finished nursing from one breast, try burping her. You will soon find out which position works best. If your baby doesn't burp after a minute or two and seems content, she probably does not need to burp.

Positions to try:

Sitting
- sit your baby sideways on your lap
- cup your thumb and first finger under her chin to support her head and use the rest of your hand to support her chest
- support her back with your other hand
- gently rock your baby back and forth and lightly rub or pat her back until you hear a burp

On the shoulder
- hold your baby upright with her head peeking over your shoulder
- support her head and back with your hand
- gently rub or pat her back until you hear a burp

On the lap
- lay your baby on her tummy on your lap
- gently rub or pat her back until you hear a burp

Taking Care of Yourself

Nutrition
- When breastfeeding, follow *Canada's Food Guide to Healthy Eating* for breastfeeding and pregnant women. Drink lots of water to satisfy your thirst.

- Whenever you are breastfeeding, have a glass of water, milk, soup, or juice within reach.

- You may continue to take a multivitamin if you choose.

Rest
- You will be up during the night to feed your baby so rest whenever possible.

- Breastfeeding takes time. Don't take on too many activities and responsibilities other than caring for your baby.

Sucking is important for feeding, comfort, stress release, and pleasure for babies. Your baby may suck on her hand, fingers, or thumb.

Alcohol and Street Drugs

Alcohol may affect your baby's sleep or decrease the amount of milk your baby takes at feeding time. It's best not to drink at all while breastfeeding. However, if you choose to have a drink, feed your baby first. Since breast milk is so good for your baby, you do not need to stop breastfeeding if you have a drink. Alcohol is not trapped in breast milk. It is continually circulated into and out of breast milk.

If you are taking street drugs or drinking alcohol in large amounts, do not breastfeed. These substances pass through your breast milk and can affect your baby. Talk with your doctor, pharmacist, health care practitioner, public health nurse, or the BC NurseLine, at 1-866-215-4700, about getting help. The Motherisk Alcohol and Substance Use Helpline can be reached at 1-877-327-4636.

The Alcohol and Drug Information Referral Service has information regarding drug and alcohol programs. Call them toll-free at 1-800-663-1441.

Being Healthy

If you get sick with the cold or flu, you should continue to breastfeed.

Before taking any prescription or non-prescription medications — including natural health products — speak with your doctor or pharmacist. Some medications will pass into the breast milk. While some are safe, others are not. Check to be sure that all your medications are safe to take while breastfeeding.

Keeping Breasts Healthy

- Wash your hands before handling your breasts.

- Express a bit of milk onto your nipples and allow them to air dry after each feeding.

- If you wear nursing pads, change them as soon as they are wet.

- Be sure your bra fits well.

- If your bra leaves a mark on your breast tissue, it is too tight. A good estimate is to buy a bra two sizes larger than you normally wear.

- If the nipple is too sore to breastfeed, express or pump your milk.

Most mothers have sore nipples in the first week. However, if your nipples are damaged — cracked, bleeding, scabbed or blistered — talk with your public health nurse, midwife, or lactation consultant about your baby's latch. It may help to nurse on the least sore side first.

What should I do if I have full, heavy, painful breasts (engorgement)?

This usually occurs after your milk increases between the third or fourth day. It may also happen if you miss a feeding. The nipples are often flattened against a swollen, sore breast. This condition usually doesn't last long and can be avoided by feeding early and frequently.

To help:
- Feed your baby at least every two to three hours. Night-time feedings are important.

- Before feeding, take a shower or place warm wet washcloths on your breasts. Massage your breasts as well.

- Soften the nipple area by expressing a small amount of milk before feeding in order to help the baby latch on.

- Position and latch your baby correctly.

- Express some milk from your breasts if they are still full and painful after feeding your baby. Make sure both breasts are well drained at least once a day.

- Apply ice packs or a bag of frozen peas to your breasts after feedings. Place a cloth between you and the ice pack.

- Chilled, washed, and dried raw cabbage leaves can also be placed on your breasts or inside your bra for comfort.

- Get as much rest as possible and drink water, milk, or juice when you are thirsty.

What causes a red sore area in a breast?
This may be a plugged duct. This can occur when a duct is not fully emptied often enough. Pressure builds up behind the duct and can cause soreness in the surrounding area. Plugged ducts can become infected. With continued nursing, plugged ducts usually clear up in 24 to 48 hours.

To relieve plugged ducts:
- Breastfeed every two to three hours. Sucking will help relieve the plugged duct.

- Before feeding, take a shower or place warm, wet washcloths on your breasts.

- Massage your breast before the feeding. During feeding, firmly massage the breast from behind the lumpy area towards the nipple area to help the milk come out of the breast.

- Change the baby's nursing position to encourage proper drainage.

- Drain one breast well before switching sides.

- Express the milk from your breasts by hand or with a pump if they are still lumpy after feeding.

- Get as much rest as possible and drink whenever you are thirsty.

- Make sure your clothing and bra are loose.

Mastitis
If you develop a fever greater than 38°C, feel as though you are getting the flu, or your breast is red and sore, you may have mastitis. Continue to breastfeed. Mastitis is an infection of the breast tissue and/or milk ducts. It may come on suddenly and make you feel sick with chills and aches. The breast may feel firm, swollen, hot, and painful and may appear red or have red streaking. If you think you have mastitis, contact your health care practitioner or the BC NurseLine (1-866-215-4700) immediately.

Mastitis can be treated with frequent feedings, antibiotics, and pain relievers. Rest is extremely important in treating mastitis. Keep the breast well emptied by breastfeeding and expressing milk frequently if necessary. Your baby will not get sick from this infection.

Thrush
If you have red, itching, persistent sore nipples, burning or shooting pain in the breast during and after feeding, or cracked nipples that don't heal, you may have thrush or a yeast infection. Both the mother and the baby may show signs of infection, or just one may show signs.

Your baby may refuse to breastfeed, may repeatedly pull off the breast during feedings, be gassy and cranky, and have slow weight gain. The baby may have thrush in the mouth (white patchy areas that look like milk that won't rub off) or in the diaper area (red rash).

If you have thrush, both you and your baby need to be treated. See your health care practitioner as soon as possible. Antifungal creams are used to help clear up thrush. Wash bras daily and avoid using breast pads if possible. If you are using a breast pump, boil the parts daily.

If you have chosen to use a soother for your baby, replace or boil the soother for two minutes each day to prevent re-infecting your baby's mouth.

Babies need a prescription for antifungals. Mothers can use non-prescription medications.

The best piece of advice I would give for breastfeeding is to be persistent. Don't give up if you have problems. There are many supports out there to help with breastfeeding and it is so worthwhile. I loved breastfeeding all of my babies. When they woke at night, it was so much easier to have their food warm and ready just when they needed it.

Getting Help with Breastfeeding

A new baby can be overwhelming and exhausting. It is important to have people around you to talk to or help with your concerns. If you are having difficulties with breastfeeding, such as sore nipples, or are tired or having emotional difficulties, call for help right away. Your public health office or the BC NurseLine can help with breastfeeding questions. Many health offices and hospitals have breastfeeding clinics where you can go and have a nurse help you while feeding. If you have a midwife, she will help you with breastfeeding. The La Leche League is also a valuable resource.

Using a Bottle or Cup
Once they have settled into a breastfeeding routine after four to six weeks, some mothers introduce an occasional cup or bottle of pumped breast milk. Remember to empty your breast if you have missed a feeding. This milk can be stored for future use.

If the baby is getting several bottles a day on a regular basis and your milk supply decreases because the baby is nursing less, it is possible that the baby will start refusing the breast, even if he is very well established in breastfeeding.

Expressing Breast Milk

You may want to express breast milk:
- If your baby is unable to breastfeed (ill or in the special care nursery).

- If you are going to be away from your baby for longer than a few hours.

- To relieve full breasts so your baby can latch better.

- If you are going back to work.

- So your partner can feed the baby after 4 to 6 weeks when your milk supply is well established.

How can you express breast milk?
- by hand
- with a hand pump
- by an electric pump

All bottles, containers, and pump pieces used for expressing milk should be washed and cleaned daily before use until your baby is three months old.

Before cleaning all bottles, containers, and pump pieces:
- wash hands well
- take pump pieces apart so each piece can be cleaned separately
- rinse milk off all pump pieces using cold water
- wash in hot, soapy water and rinse well
- air dry by placing on a paper towel

If your baby is preterm or ill, you will also need to disinfect the pump parts once a day. Use **one** of these methods:
- Put pump parts in a pot, cover with water, and boil on the stove for 10 minutes.

- Soak pump parts for 10 minutes in household bleach. Use 250 ml (1 cup) of bleach and 2.25 litres (10 cups) of tap water. Rinse with boiled water. Air dry.

- Use the sani cycle on your dishwasher. Place pump parts on the top rack.

When your milk supply is first coming in, you may only get a few drops when you express. This will increase as you practice and your milk supply increases. If you express milk for a preterm or sick baby, or a baby having difficulty breastfeeding, express or pump for every feeding (eight times in 24 hours). If you are expressing to get extra milk for a feeding when you will be away, you may need to express milk several times to get enough milk for one feeding. Find the time that works best for you. You may feel fullest in the morning, so this is a good time to try to express your milk.

You can tuck a small (non-breakable) container under your nipple on the second breast while your baby is nursing. You may find you leak milk from both breasts when you have the let-down reflex. Save this milk for use later.

Hand Expressing

- Wash your hands and get comfortable.

- Have a clean cup, bowl, or jar ready to catch the milk.

- Gently massage your breast in a circular motion, working from shoulder to nipple.

- To start the let-down reflex, roll your nipple between your thumb and finger.

- Put your hand in a C-shape on your breast. Put fingers on the bottom and your thumb on the top at the outer edge of the areola.

Expressing milk by hand.

- Gently push your thumb and fingers back towards your chest, then squeeze them together while you move them towards the nipple, but do not pinch your nipple.

- Catch the milk in the clean cup, bowl, or jar.

- Move your fingers around the areola in a circle to express from different parts of your breast. Press and release, repeat the movement on your breast, and switch between breasts every few minutes.

Hand Pumps
Some women like to use hand pumps. These pumps can usually be bought in a drug store or child care supply stores.

Electric pumps
Electric pumps are fast and efficient. They are useful if you will be expressing milk often or for a longer period of time. You are able to express both breasts at the same time with some electric pumps. Electric pumps that suck and release automatically work best. Many mothers find that pumps requiring them to create and release the suction with their fingers do not work well. Talk with the nurses in the hospital or your public health nurse about renting or buying an electric pump.

Collecting and Storing Breast Milk
Store your expressed breast milk for:
- Up to 4 hours at room temperature.

- 3 days in a fridge that has a temperature of 0 to 4°C. Store in the refrigerator, not in the door. If you don't have a fridge thermometer, it is best to freeze milk you don't intend to use within 24 hours.

- 1 month in a freezer compartment that is inside a fridge.

- Up to 6 months in a separate-door fridge freezer (the temperature changes if the door is opened often). Keep milk on the back top shelf at a temperature of -18°C.

- 6 to 12 months in a deep freeze (-20°C).

Points to Remember

Do you have too much milk? Consider contacting the BC Women's Milk Bank at BC Women's Hospital and Health Centre.

Call 604-875-2282 to find out about the screening process to become a milk donor.

How do I use frozen breast milk safely?
Always use the oldest milk first. Breast milk can separate when it is frozen. Gently shake to remix once it thaws.

Thaw breast milk by:
- putting the container in the fridge
- running the container under warm tap water
- putting the container in a bowl of warm water

Once milk has thawed, it may be refrigerated for up to 24 hours. Do not store at room temperature. Avoid wasting thawed breast milk. Thaw only what you need for one feeding.

Do not refreeze breast milk.

Do not heat breast milk on top of the stove. It can get too hot too fast.

Do not microwave breast milk because the uneven heating can burn your baby's mouth.

Warm breast milk by:
- running the container under warm tap water (if using an infant bottle, keep the nipple area out of the water)
- putting the container in a bowl of warm water

Formula Feeding

It is rare that a woman is unable to or advised not to breastfeed her baby. If you are unsure about breastfeeding or are considering formula feeding, talk first with your health care practitioner or phone the BC NurseLine at 1-866-215-4700. They have many ways to help you with breastfeeding.

Do not give ordinary cow's milk, goat's milk, or soy drink to babies younger than 9 to 12 months. These milks can hurt your baby's stomach and kidneys.

Information on formula feeding your baby is available from HealthFile #68l, which can be picked up at your public health office or viewed online at www.bchealthguide.org. You can also call Dial-a-Dietitian or the BC NurseLine (see Resources section for phone numbers).

Breastfeeding and Work

You can breastfeed and work outside the home. In British Columbia, employers must make reasonable efforts to allow you to breastfeed or express milk at work.

How can you be successful?
- Have breastfeeding well established before returning to work. The first six weeks or more are the most important for getting a good milk supply for your baby.

- Contact your public health nurse, lactation consultant, La Leche League, or breastfeeding support group for help and advice.

- Talk to your boss before you go back to work. Talk about the importance of support for breastfeeding. Breastfed babies are healthier. Their mothers need less time off work to care for sick babies.

You will need:
- A quiet, smoke-free place to feed or express milk.

- A fridge to store expressed milk. If you don't have a fridge at work, use a Styrofoam box with an ice pack to store expressed milk that will be fed to your baby within 24 hours.

- A reasonable workload.

To keep enough breast milk, you will need to pump your breasts or feed your baby one to three times during an eight-hour work shift.

Remember to take healthy snacks to work, as well as breast pads, breast pump, clean cups or jars to store your breast milk, and phone numbers of support people.

How can I get ready to go back to work?

- Learn how to express your milk by hand or pump. Start storing milk 10 to 14 days before you plan to return to work.

- About two weeks before you go back to work, slowly introduce your baby to other ways of feeding. Let your baby get used to a cup or bottle. It may help if someone other than you feeds the baby at these times. If you use a bottle and your baby refuses the nipple, try a different nipple or a cup.

- Breastfeed as soon as you see your baby after work and breastfeed often on your days off, in the evening, and at night.

- Your baby may refuse food, wake at night, or be fussier when you are away.

- Tell your child care provider how important breastfeeding is to you and your baby. Talk about when you will be gone, when you will breastfeed your baby, and about your baby's feeding routines. Make sure your caregiver knows how to safely prepare and store milk.

- Get extra help with chores at home.

- Breastfeeding helps your baby adjust to you going back to work.

Vitamin D Supplement

Health Canada recommends that all breastfed, healthy, full term babies get a daily vitamin D supplement of 400 IU per day. You should start giving your baby vitamin D supplement at birth. Continue giving it until your baby's foods include 400 IU of vitamin D each day.

- Your baby needs vitamin D to build strong, healthy bones and teeth.

- Not enough vitamin D increases the risk of your baby getting rickets — a disease that affects the way bones grow and develop.

Vitamin D and Sunlight

Sunlight is the main source of vitamin D for all humans, but wearing sunscreen prevents vitamin D from being formed. Canada's northern location and our use of sunscreen to lessen the risk of skin cancer means we can't count on getting enough vitamin D from being in the sun. Children and adults can get additional vitamin D from foods. See BC HealthFile #68e, *Food Sources of Calcium and Vitamin D* at www.bchealthguide.org.

- Infants under one year should be kept out of direct sunlight.

- Sunscreen should not be used on babies less than 6 months of age.

- For infants over 6 months who are exposed to sunlight, sunscreen is recommended.

Feeding the First Solid Foods

Your baby does not need any food except breast milk for the first six months. Babies should be able to sit up with some support, open their mouths when they see food coming, and move the soft food from the front of the tongue to the back of the mouth to swallow. If you wait until your baby can do these things, your baby will feel more confident about learning to eat and will give you signals about hunger, fullness, likes, and dislikes by turning her head away. Infants who start solid foods too early have a greater chance of developing food allergies.

Baby Care

Sleeping

For the first month, your baby may sleep for about 15 hours of every 24 hours. She will usually not sleep longer than two or three hours at a time. In the early days it is common for babies to wake up several times at night. Getting enough sleep can be a big issue for many parents. Breastfeeding is the best way to get your baby back to sleep. Over time, your baby will gradually sleep longer during the night.

Here are a few tips:

- Have a clear difference between daytime and nighttime sleeping. When you are up at night to feed your baby, keep the room darkened and don't turn on the TV or radio. Try not to play with or stimulate your baby before putting him back down to sleep. During the daytime, let your baby sleep in a lightened room with normal daytime noises. In the daytime sing to him, play, and generally get on with your day.

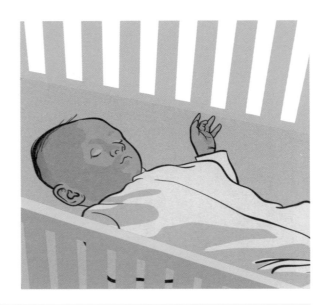

Is Baby Too Warm or Too Cold?

The best guide for how many clothes or blankets a baby needs is to dress your baby as you would dress yourself. Your baby needs to be comfortably warm or cool, depending on the temperature outside and inside your house.

In the house, babies need about the same number of layers of clothes as an adult to stay warm. When putting your baby to sleep, it is recommended that you use a sleeper and a light blanket or a blanket-weight sleeper. Keep your baby's head uncovered when sleeping. This is so your baby does not get too hot. Avoid using heavy blankets, quilts, and duvets.

If your baby is overdressed or is wrapped in too many blankets, she may develop a rash that looks like clusters of tiny pink pimples surrounded by pink skin. Your baby may also get sleepy and sweaty.

Infants who are too cold will usually fuss until the problem is fixed. Cold hands and feet don't necessarily mean that the baby is cold. Feel the warmth on the upper arms or thighs. Add a sweater or a light blanket.

A large portion of an infant's body surface area is on their heads. In other words, their heads are large in comparison to their bodies. Because of this, they can lose a lot of heat through their heads. When outdoors, it is wise to use a hat to keep your baby warm when the weather is cool. In summer, protect your baby's head from the sun by using a light hat.

- Have enough nap time during the day. An over-tired baby will not sleep better at night.

- Make sure your baby is warm but not hot.

- Put your baby to sleep in a safe sleeping environment.

- Have a routine that you follow at night. This may not be possible in the first few months. As your baby gets older, have a warm bath at night followed by rocking or singing and quiet time. This routine signals to your baby that sleep is coming.

Safety and Sleeping

Safe Sleeping for You And Your Baby
You need to carefully choose where your baby sleeps. There are many ways to help you and your baby sleep well and safely.

Co-sleeping refers to the sleeping arrangement where the infant sleeps in the same room as a parent, but not in the same bed.

Bedsharing means the baby shares the same sleep surface with another person, usually a parent. In many areas of the world it is a common practice for mothers to sleep with their babies so they can watch them, breastfeed them, and be near them. Sometimes you may decide to have your baby sleep beside your bed and at other times have your baby share your bed.

You need to know the benefits and risks of co-sleeping and bedsharing, and consider them each time you choose where your baby sleeps. Having your baby in bed with you makes breastfeeding easier and your baby can feed more often. It is best to put your baby on his back when not breastfeeding. Having your baby share your room, particularly at night, may help lower the risk of Sudden Infant Death Syndrome (SIDS). Being close can also help to calm your baby if he is unsettled.

The Canadian Pediatric Society (CPS) released recommendations in 2004 that discourage bedsharing for the first year of life. Sharing a bed with your baby can increase your risk of smothering your baby, especially if you are very tired or have been drinking alcohol or using drugs. The CPS also knows that some parents will choose to share a bed with their baby.

You should **not** share a bed with your baby if you (or any other person in the bed):
- are a smoker, or your baby is exposed to second-hand smoke
- have been drinking alcohol or using drugs
- have taken any medicines that could make you extra sleepy
- are very tired, to the point where you would not be able to respond to your baby
- are ill or have a medical condition that might make it difficult to respond to your baby
- have long hair that is not tied back
- are unusually heavy (obese)

There are other things you need to know when choosing where your baby sleeps:
- **It is safest to put your baby on his back to sleep. This is very important!**

- Your baby should sleep on a firm, flat mattress. Do not put your baby to sleep on a waterbed, sagging mattress, feather bed, air mattress, sofa, couch, daybed, or any other surface that is very soft.

- Be sure your baby will not fall out of bed. There should be no spaces between the mattress and the headboard, walls, or other surfaces that can trap your baby.

- Do not sleep with your baby while sitting or lying on a sofa, recliner, or chair. Your baby could fall between the cushions and suffocate, or fall on the floor.

- Make sure your baby does not get too warm. Use only a light blanket to cover him. Do not swaddle or wrap your sleeping baby tightly in a blanket or cover his head.

Do not swaddle (wrap snugly in a blanket) or cover your baby's head with the blanket if you have your baby in bed with you.

Do not use:
- sheep skins
- pillows
- comforters
- stuffed toys
- bumper pads

These things can stop good air circulation around your baby's face. Plastics, such as the mattress wrapping, may also prevent air circulation. These should be removed to reduce the risk of SIDS and suffocation.

Do not let your baby sleep on:
- waterbeds
- couches or sofas
- recliner chairs
- pillows
- down comforters
- beanbag chairs

- Do not put your baby down to sleep on or beside a pillow.

- Use a crib that meets safety standards and don't use bumper pads, sheepskins, or comforters, or have stuffed toys in the crib.

- Do not leave your baby alone on an adult bed or let other children sleep in the same bed as your baby.

SIDS (Sudden Infant Death Syndrome)

SIDS, also known as crib death, is the sudden and unexpected death of a healthy baby. No one can explain why a baby dies of SIDS but there are steps you can take to lessen the risk.

- **Babies should sleep on their backs on a firm surface.**

- When your baby can turn over on his own, there is no need to continue to place your baby in the back sleep position. When your baby is awake, allow some tummy time to help develop arm and neck strength. See page 121 for more information on tummy time.

- **No one should smoke inside your home.** A smoke-free home is important — not only for your baby's health but also to reduce the risk of SIDS.

- Keep your baby warm, not hot. To check if your baby is too hot, place your hand on the back of the neck. Your baby should not be sweating.

- Breastfeeding may help to prevent SIDS.

Sleeping Equipment

What do I need to know about cribs?

Your baby can sleep in a crib, cradle, bassinet, basket, or even a box as long as the surface is firm and not soft. When your baby becomes active you may find that a crib is needed.

Only use cribs that meet the federal government's *Cribs and Cradles Regulations*. Be sure that each part of the crib is

properly and securely in place at all times. Follow the manufacturer's instructions when putting the crib together. Cribs should also have double locks for securing the drop side. Check for the manufacture date — most cribs made before 1986 do not meet current safety regulations. For more information, see the Canadian Health Network website at www.canadian-health-network.ca and search for "cribs."

What do I need to know about mattresses?

The mattress should be firm, no more than 15 cm (6 inches) thick, fit the frame properly, have no gaps greater than 3 cm (1 1/8 inches) along the sides or ends of the crib. If spaces are larger than this, your baby can get his head stuck in any gaps between the mattress and the frame and suffocate. If the mattress is worn or has a tear, it is dangerous. Do not use it. The mattress support should hold firmly and be checked often. You can do this by shaking the mattress support, thumping the mattress from the top, and pushing hard on the support from underneath. Make sure all screws, locks, and clamps are tight.

What do I need to know about bedding?

- To protect the crib mattress, you can use either a quilted crib pad (one side waterproof) or a mattress cover, placed under the sheets. Do not use plastic sheets as they can get in the way of breathing.

- Pillowcases can be used as a bottom sheet for a bassinet or carriage mattress.

- Have some bottom sheets (can be fitted) for the crib mattress.

- In a warm room, a sleeper and a light blanket or a blanket-weight sleeper should be enough to keep your baby comfortable.

- Your baby should be warm but not hot.

- Top sheets are not recommended until your child is an older toddler. Babies can get tangled in a top sheet.

- Never cover your baby's face or head with blankets.

Diapering

Your newborn baby may need her diaper changed 10 to15 times a day. Since you will spend a lot of time doing this, make it a special time for talking, laughing, and playing with your baby. You do not need to wake your baby to change her diaper.

Tips for Diapering

- Wash your hands before and after each change.

- Put your baby on a flat, safe surface, such as a change table with side rails or on the floor.

- Keep one hand on your baby at all times.

- Babies move around, so keep creams, pins, etc., out of reach. Give your baby a toy or something to watch to keep her entertained.

- Wipe the diaper area with a warm wet washcloth or baby wipe (one that does not have perfume).

- Pat the area dry or allow it to air dry.

- Safety pins pushed into a bar of soap are easier to pin into the diaper.

- Do not use powder or cornstarch. A puff of powder near the face or nostrils can cause choking and breathing difficulty.

Your pregnancy hormones may have caused some changes in your baby's body after birth. A girl's genitals may look larger than normal and you might see a small amount of bleeding or white discharge from the vagina. Boys may have a reddened scrotum. Breasts in both boys and girls may be larger than normal and may even leak a small amount of milk. These changes are normal and will go away in a few days.

How do I diaper and clean a girl?

Wipe from the front to the back to prevent germs from her bowel movements getting into the urinary tract. Gently clean between the outer folds of the labia. There is no need to clean inside the vagina.

How do I diaper and clean a boy?

Do not pull the foreskin back when cleaning the penis. Pulling this skin back may cause infection or tightening of the foreskin. Wash the area well and clean from the front to the back.

What is diaper rash?

This is a red and painful rash on the diaper area. Rashes can be caused by:

- Irritation from dampness of urine or bowel movement on the skin.

- Allergic reaction to soaps, perfumes, or oils that touch the skin.

- Yeast infection that can be spread from the mouth or from stool. A yeast infection can develop after your baby has had a rash for several days.

Hints to Avoid Diaper Rash

- Wash your hands before and after changing diapers.

- Keep the skin dry by changing diapers as soon as they are wet or soiled.

- Wash the diaper area with warm water and dry well. Do not use soap.

- Take the diaper off and expose the area to the air for 10 to 15 minutes, three or four times a day. You can lay your baby on an absorbent towel and play with her during this time.

- When the diaper area is clean and dry, rub on a thin layer of petroleum jelly or zinc-based cream.

To prevent burns, keep the temperature of your hot water tank below
49°C (120°F).

- Avoid using perfumed fabric softeners or baby care products like diaper wipes (purchased diaper wipes may cause or further irritate diaper rash).

- If you use cloth diapers you may want to do an extra rinse when washing the diapers or use an antibacterial product or vinegar in the wash. This will decrease the ammonia build up in the diapers caused by urine.

- Avoid using airtight plastic pants over the diaper.

- Try switching to cloth diapers if you are using disposables and the rash is getting worse.

Contact your health care practitioner if you have followed these suggestions and the rash lasts longer than five days, has blisters, pus, peeling areas or crusty patches, or is mainly in the skin creases.

Choosing Diapers

Your baby will be in diapers for two to three years. Consider these factors when making your choice.

Disposable diapers:
- do not need to be worn with waterproof pants
- will cost more than cloth diapers
- come in a number of styles and sizes
- are convenient, no laundering is needed
- create a lot of extra garbage

Cloth diapers:
- can be made or bought
- can be fastened with diaper pins or Velcro fasteners
- will need to be worn with waterproof pants
- can be cleaned by a diaper service that picks up soiled diapers and leaves clean ones

Washing Diapers

- Diapers may be soaked in a diaper pail until there are enough to be washed.

- Fill the diaper pail three-quarters full of water and add 175 millilitres (3/4 cup) of vinegar (not bleach).

- Rinse soiled diapers in the toilet. Wet diapers do not need to be rinsed.

- If you use diaper pail deodorizing tablets, you must keep the pail out of reach of your children.

- When the diaper pail is full, empty the contents into the washing machine and spin out the excess water.

- Fill the machine with hot water to the highest water level.

- Use a phosphate-free detergent or biodegradable soap. Run diapers through an extra rinse at the end of the cycle.

- Dry diapers in the dryer on a hot setting or hang outside to dry. Many diapers will stay softer if put in a dryer for 15 minutes, then hung outside on a line or rail to finish drying.

Bathing

You don't need to bathe your baby every day. Washing the face, neck, hands, and diaper area, in that order and with attention to skin folds, can be done daily. Your baby may love the bath or cry when he is naked. Most babies usually relax when they are floating in the water. Don't worry, you are not harming your baby. If you are calm and talk gently, your baby will get used to the routine and start to enjoy the bath. For the first bath it helps to have someone with you who has done it before. Try to make bath time a relaxed playful experience for your baby. Smile, make eye contact, sing, and talk with your baby.

Never leave your baby alone in the bath.

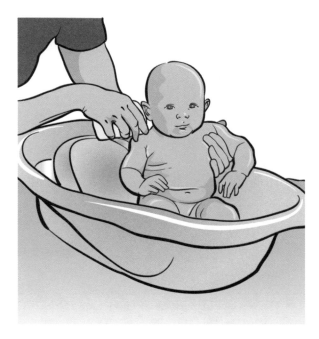

General Tips for Bathing

- Have the room warm, about 22 to 27°C (72 to 80°F).

- Remove jewellery that could scratch your baby.

- Wash your hands.

- A baby can have a bath in the sink, a basin, a baby bathtub, or in a bathtub with an adult.

- Lay out a blanket or towel next to the sink, basin, or baby bathtub to lay your baby on.

- Bath water should be lukewarm. Check the temperature of the water on your wrist or elbow. It should feel warm, not hot.

- Have everything within easy reach before you start.

- Always keep at least one hand on your baby when in the bath or on the table.

- Using oils in the bath can make your baby slippery. Apply any oils you may want to use after the bath.

- When washing, think cleanest to dirtiest. Wash the eyes and face first.

Eyes and Face

- Wash the face using warm water only. Soap is not needed on this area.

- Wipe eyes from inner corner to the outer corner.

- Do not use cotton tipped applicators in your baby's ears, nose, or eyes as they can harm the delicate tissues.

- Use a soft washcloth, and only clean the outer part of the ear. Don't dig into the ear canal.

- Wipe your baby's gums with a soft clean cloth every day.

Scalp and Hair

- You can use a mild soap or baby shampoo. Lather up and rinse well with clear water.

- Your baby's scalp is normally mildly scaly. If the scalp is crusty you can rub in a small amount of non-perfumed oil, then wash if off. Oil left on the scalp can cause a build-up of oil and skin known as cradle cap.

Umbilical Cord

- The umbilical cord stump will usually fall off in 5 to 15 days.

- Keeping the cord clean and dry is important to prevent infection.

- Use water on a cotton-tipped applicator or washcloth to clean gently around the base of the cord. Wipe away any cord discharge.

- Clean around the base of the cord after bathing and at diaper changes.

Points to Remember

Health Canada recommends that parents not use bath seats or rings because of concerns with their safety. It is very easy for an infant to tip over or slip underwater and drown. This can happen in less than a minute.

Points to Remember

Another way to bathe your baby—have one adult sit in a bathtub while the other passes the baby in for a bath. When the bath is finished, the baby can be passed to the other adult. Your baby may feel more secure and cry less.

Points to Remember

Call your health care practitioner if:

- The skin around your baby's umbilical cord is warm, red, or swollen.

- There is a bad-smelling discharge from the cord.

- The cord is very wet and will not dry with exposure to air.

If a rash flares up and becomes red, itchy, and oozes fluid, call your health care practitioner. For more information on checking the seriousness of a rash and knowing when to call a doctor, look in the *BC HealthGuide* handbook. You can also visit BC HealthGuide OnLine at www.bchealthguide.org and search for "rashes." Or you can call the BC NurseLine at 1-866-215-4700 for confidential help and advice.

- Fold the diaper below the cord to stop irritation and to keep it dry and exposed to air.

- Continue to clean the belly button (umbilicus) for a few days after the cord falls off.

The cord may be infected if the area around the cord becomes reddened, swollen, or has pus coming from it. Call your health care practitioner or the public health nurse if you are concerned.

Diaper Area
Wash this area last as it will be the least clean.

Drying
After you have bathed your baby, place her on the towel and pat her dry, being sure to remember the skin folds. Your baby will cool down quickly when wet. Have warm clothes ready to dress her.

Caring for Baby's Skin

A newborn's skin is usually soft and smooth but may be peeling or wrinkled in the first few days after birth.

What are the tiny white raised dots on my baby's face?
These spots are called milia. Your hormones before birth cause extra oil gland activity in your baby. Milia are caused by plugged oil glands and will usually clear within three to four weeks. Do not try to remove or pop these glands.

Do I need to treat newborn rash?
Newborn rash is common in the first few months after birth. This rash is blotchy red with tiny pinpoints that can be found anywhere on the body. The cause is unknown. It's normal and will pass on its own with no treatment.

What can I do to avoid rashes on my baby?
- Remove your baby's extra clothing. Keep him warm but not hot.

- Don't use perfumed soaps, lotions, or fabric softeners.

- Bathe your baby every second or third day. Keep the baths short and the water lukewarm, not hot. Water and soap can dry and irritate the skin.

- Dress your baby in 100% cotton.

- Use plain non-medicated, unscented skin lotions or oils to keep the skin moist.

Caring for Baby's Nails

Keeping your baby's nails trimmed will help prevent your baby from scratching himself.

- Use blunt scissors or an emery board to cut or file your baby's nails.

- The best time to do your baby's nails is when he is asleep or at least sleepy and his hands are open and still.

Jaundice

Jaundice appears in about half of full term babies and about three-quarters of preterm babies. Following birth, your baby has extra red blood cells. As the blood cells break down, a yellow-coloured substance called bilirubin is released. The yellow-coloured substance in the baby's blood causes the skin and the whites of the eyes to take on a yellowish tinge called jaundice.

In most infants, jaundice is mild. It comes on during the first three to five days and lasts only a few days. The only treatment needed is lots of breastfeeding. Your baby may be a little sleepier and may need to be woken on a regular basis — every three hours — for feeding. The extra milk will help get rid of the bilirubin. To help with jaundice, feed your baby as often and for as long as she wants. Do not give water by bottle as bilirubin is better eliminated through stools than urine. Water will only fill up the tummy and decrease breastfeeding. This will decrease the number of stools.

In rare cases, jaundice is severe. Untreated severe jaundice can lead to brain damage and deafness. With higher levels of jaundice, your baby still needs lots of breastfeeding. He will be placed under special lights to get rid of bilirubin.

Call your health care practitioner if:

- Your baby seems sleepy and refuses the breast or bottle.

- You notice your newborn is jaundiced, especially on his arms and legs.

Bowel Movements

Normal Stools

For the first week after birth, the appearance of your baby's stool will change every day. Usually within the first 24 hours after birth, your baby will pass her first bowel movement, called meconium. This first stool will be thick, dark, greenish-black, sticky, and tar-like, and have no smell. The next stool is called transitional stool. It will be looser and greenish-brown. After the meconium has passed, your baby's stools will vary, depending on how your baby is fed. If your baby is less than two weeks old and has fewer than two stools per day, contact your health care practitioner or public health nurse.

Stools of Breastfed Babies

After the third or fourth day, the stool will tend to be soft and golden-yellow (mustard) coloured. The stools will be soft and runny with a curdled or seed-like appearance. They will not smell. Breastfed babies often pass a stool after each feeding. After day four, your baby should have at least three to four stools about the size of a loonie or one large stool every 24 hours in the first weeks. After the first month, bowel movements happen less often. Breast milk leaves very little waste in the intestines so bowel movements may come only once every few days to once a week. Almost all infants will grunt and turn red when passing a stool. If your baby is totally breastfed, he will not be constipated.

Stools of Formula Fed Babies

Formula-fed infants pass stools that are pasty and pudding-like. They are pale-yellow to light brown with a strong odor. Formula-fed newborns usually have one to two bowel movements daily in the first weeks. After the first month your baby may have a bowel movement every one to two days. It is important to know that almost all infants will grunt and turn red when passing a stool. If you think your child is having a hard time passing a stool, contact your health care practitioner.

Constipation

A baby who is completely breastfed rarely gets constipated. Breast milk is almost totally digested. After the first few weeks, a fully breastfed baby may go as long as a week between bowel movements. Newborns and infants may grunt and get red in the face when having a bowel movement. This does not mean they are constipated. Babies differ in how often they have bowel movements. After the first few weeks, some newborns will have stools every day. Others will go for days without a bowel movement. Constipation may be evident if stools are dry and hard or if your baby has difficulty passing them.

If constipation continues for more than a week, or if there is fresh blood in the baby's stools, see your health care practitioner or call the BC NurseLine or Dial-A-Dietitian (see the Resources section for phone numbers). Do not use laxatives, suppositories, or enemas unless a doctor prescribes them.

Urination (Peeing)

When and how much should my baby pee?

Your baby may pee either immediately after birth or several hours later. Most newborns will pee within 24 hours of birth. In the first three days of life, one to two wet diapers per day are normal. By days four to six, as your milk supply increases, your baby should have five or more very wet diapers per day.

Urine will be pale and may be difficult to see. To tell if your baby has peed:

- feel how heavy the diaper is compared to a dry one
- a tissue or paper towel can be used inside a disposable diaper to see if it becomes wet
- cut the disposable diaper and feel if it is wet

It is common to find a pink stain on the diapers. A rusty orange stain may also be seen on the diaper in the first one to three days after birth. This stain is caused by uric acid crystals in the urine. If you notice these crystals after the fourth day, feed your baby more often.

Call your health care practitioner or the BC NurseLine's 24-hour toll free number at 1-866-215-4700 if:

- the uric acid crystals continue
- urine is bloody or the colour of cola
- there is little or no urine for 8 hours

Diarrhea

Diarrhea is often caused by an infection or some other illness or irritation. Diarrhea is different from normal stools. Diarrhea stools are watery and foul smelling. Diarrhea can cause dehydration. Babies can become very sick, very quickly.

Most cases of mild diarrhea can be treated at home. Your baby should be taking in enough fluids and nutrients and be peeing normal amounts and seem to be improving. If your baby has signs of dehydration, see your health care practitioner right away.

What are the signs of dehydration?
- has less than 4 wet diapers in 24 hours
- dry mouth and tongue
- a sunken front fontanel or soft spot on their head
- grey skin colour

Vomiting

Vomiting involves the forceful throwing up of large amounts of liquid. Vomiting is usually caused by a virus or bacteria. It can lead to dehydration. See your health care practitioner if your baby is unable to keep any fluids down or appears dehydrated.

Coughing and Sneezing

Babies clear their nasal passages by coughing and sneezing. This is common in newborns and does not mean they have a cold. It is uncommon for a newborn to develop a cold within the first six weeks. If you are concerned, check with your health care practitioner. You can also call the BC NurseLine for helpful information and advice on when to see a health care practitioner.

Dental Care

Did you know?
Tooth decay is an infectious disease caused by bacteria in the mouth. Babies are not born with the bacteria that cause decay. These germs can be passed from parent to baby by kissing, sharing spoons, tasting food or putting the baby's soother in your mouth. If either parent has tooth decay, see your dentist. Good dental care can help to prevent passing bacteria onto your baby.

Once babies have their first teeth, allowing them to have bottles during the day for long periods or during sleep times (naps and overnight) can lead to tooth decay.

To learn more about baby dental care, go to BC HealthFile #19a, *Infant Dental Care* at www.bchealthguide.org.

How can I care for my baby's mouth?
You should start to clean your baby's mouth with a clean, wet cloth soon after birth. Find a position that is comfortable for both of you. One suggestion is to have your baby lie in your lap. Position your baby so her head is stable and you can see into her mouth.

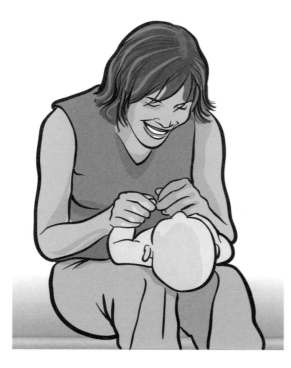

- Wipe all around your baby's gums with a clean wet cloth held over your finger.

- Once teeth appear, lift the lip so you can see along the gum line when cleaning.

- Use a soft baby toothbrush and a smear of fluoride toothpaste to clean teeth.

- Brush your baby's teeth twice a day. One brushing should be after the last feeding of the day.

- For more information on fluoride, refer to *Toddler's First Steps* and BC HealthFile #28, *Water Fluoridation Facts* at www.bchealthguide.org.

Teething

Each baby has its own schedule for teething. Once teething starts, it continues almost uninterrupted for about two years. Some babies have no difficulty with teething while others may become fussy and uncomfortable.

Some things you can do to relieve sore or tender gums:
- Give your baby a clean, chilled teething ring or cold, wet cloth to chew on.

- Clean and massage the gums regularly to ease discomfort.

- Teething gels and ointments are not recommended.

Give your baby extra love and patience to help her through the teething process.

Even though baby or first teeth are replaced by permanent teeth, your baby's first teeth are very important.

First teeth:
- Make it possible for your baby to eat solid foods.

- Play a role in helping your baby learn to speak.

- Aid in jaw development and hold the space for the permanent teeth. Your child will have some baby teeth until he is 11 to 12 years old.

Vaccinations

What are vaccinations?
Vaccinations protect your child from a disease before it has a chance to make your child sick. Other words for vaccinations are shots, needles, boosters, and immunizations.

How do vaccinations work?
Vaccinations help your baby's immune system make substances called antibodies that fight diseases. Your baby then develops protection against these diseases. With vaccinations, your baby doesn't have to get sick first to get that protection. Vaccinations work best when they are given at certain ages. For example, the measles vaccine is not given until a child is at least a year old. If it is given earlier than that, it may not work as well. Some vaccines are only given once or twice, and some need to be given over a period of time in a series of properly spaced shots.

By having your baby get his shots, you give him the best possible protection against many serious diseases.

It is important for your baby to get his shots on time. For more information you can read about various immunizations in the BC HealthFiles found at www.bchealthguide.org. You can also call the BC NurseLine, at 1-886-215-4700, and your public health office for more information about vaccines.

Why should I have my baby vaccinated?

Vaccination is the best way to protect your child against many serious diseases. Thanks to vaccinations, many diseases are not common in Canada, but in other countries the germs that cause these diseases still exist.

How can I keep my child's shots up-to-date?

It is important to keep a record of all the shots your child gets. Children in Canada are protected against dangerous diseases when they are up-to-date with their shots. Keeping a record helps you keep your child up-to-date. Ask your public health nurse for a Child Health Passport to help you keep track of your child's immunizations. Always take your child's record with you when he gets his shots. Keep it with other important papers. Your child will need his immunization record when he is older.

What diseases do vaccines protect against?

In British Columbia, vaccines protect your child against these diseases: measles, mumps, rubella, hepatitis B, diphtheria, tetanus, pertussis (whooping cough), polio, Haemophilus influenzae type b disease (Hib), chicken pox, pneumococcal, and meningococcal diseases. Without getting his shots, your child could get very sick.

Are vaccines safe?

Vaccines are very safe. Most shots cause only temporary minor side effects. These side effects might be soreness where the needle went into the arm or leg or a slight fever. These do not usually last long. Serious side effects from vaccines are very rare. Remember—if your child gets one of these diseases, the risks of the disease are far greater than the risk of a serious vaccine reaction. If you have questions about these side effects or how to make your baby more comfortable if he gets a fever or a sore arm or leg, ask your health care practitioner.

When should I have my child vaccinated?

Your child's first shots begin at two months of age. Please see the vaccine schedule below.
Remember—some vaccines are only given once or twice, and some need to be given over a period of time.

Vaccine	2 months of age	4 months of age	6 months of age	12 months of age	18 months of age	4–6 years of age
Diphtheria, Pertussis, Tetanus, Poliomyelitis, Haemophilus Influenzae Type b (Hib)	✔	✔	✔		✔	✔ (except Hib)
Hepatitis B	✔	✔	✔			
Pneumococcal Conjugate	✔	✔	✔		✔	
MMR (Measles, Mumps, and Rubella)				✔	✔	
Meningococcal C Conjugate	✔			✔		
Varicella (chicken pox)				✔		

Tummy Time

Tummy time is laying your baby on his stomach or side when he is awake. Your baby can be on the floor, on a safe firm surface, on your lap, or on your chest. It is a time when you can show toys or pictures, sing or talk, or massage your baby's back, arms and legs. Your baby should be supervised while he is on his stomach.

Having tummy time for several short periods each day helps in your baby's development. It helps:
- prevent your baby from getting a flat area on his head called *positional plagiocephaly*
- make the muscles of your baby's neck, back, and arms strong
- your baby learn to roll and crawl

A baby can get a flat area on the head because of:
- position in pregnancy or during birth
- always resting on the same area of the head (this can cause the bones of the skull to flatten)

You can help your baby have a round head shape by:
- having supervised tummy time several times a day
- avoiding long periods in bouncy seats, infant swings and strollers
- limiting the time your baby spends in a car seat
- changing the positions you use to hold and carry your baby
- changing your baby's position in the crib each day (position the baby's head at alternating ends of the crib)
- moving mobiles around the crib

Remember to place your baby on his back to sleep.

If you have questions, speak to your health care practitioner. Information is also available on these websites:
- www.cranialtech.com/medicalinfo/plagiocephaly.html
- www.cheo.on.ca

Crying

Crying is your baby's way of communicating and letting you know he needs something. If babies are tired, sick, hungry, frustrated, wet, bored, or lonely, they say so by crying. Many newborns, when they aren't eating or sleeping, spend time crying. Crying usually increases at about two weeks of age and peaks at around two months of age. At about three to four months, the long bouts of crying usually stop. It is normal for a baby to cry between one to four hours a day. Babies will often have fussy times around supper time and into the evening. This is normal. Listen to the sounds your baby makes — you will soon discover how he talks to you. Remember — it is normal for babies to move and make sounds, even when sleeping.

 He Said

I was overwhelmed by how much our baby cried. I had a hard time understanding that she would cry for not minutes at a time, but hours! We would feed, diaper, rock, and cuddle her, but sometimes nothing seemed to comfort her. The only thing that would calm her at those times would be a drive in the car. I did many trips in the evening, just driving around the neighbourhood until she would go to sleep.

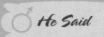
We would tag team every evening for the first three months. I would walk and rock for 20 minutes and then my partner would take over for 20 minutes. And then when we would both be worn out, my mother would take over and we would walk outside for a 20 minute break. The key for us was to not leave one person to cope alone for too long. It was definitely a team effort.

How can I soothe a crying baby?

If you think your baby is hungry or thirsty, try:
- feeding your baby, especially if it has been more than one hour since the last feeding

If you think your baby may be uncomfortable, try:
- cuddling and comforting your baby
- burping your baby
- checking for open diaper pins
- changing the diaper if it is wet or soiled
- changing your baby's position or giving your baby a gentle back rub
- checking that the room temperature isn't too warm or too cold and that your baby isn't over- or under-dressed.

To find out how to tell if your baby is too warm or too cold, see page 110.

If you think your baby may be feeling insecure, bored, or lonely, try:
- holding your baby close to your body and cuddling
- moving slowly and calmly with your baby
- smiling and making eye contact
- talking, singing, or reading to your baby
- playing soothing music
- having an interesting toy or mobile for the baby to watch
- taking your baby for a walk in a front carrier or stroller
- taking your baby into a room with other people
- rocking your baby
- wrapping your baby snugly in a light blanket and holding her

> Never take a snugly wrapped baby to bed with you. Your baby may get too warm, and needs to be able to use her arms and legs to move away from your body if needed.

If your baby is over stimulated or overtired, try:
- offering your breast

- a quiet, rhythmic motion, e.g., rocking, patting, going for a stroller or car ride
- creating a soothing background noise by turning on the dishwasher, clothes dryer, or vacuum cleaner as many babies like sounds of this sort
- moving to a quieter spot, e.g., place the baby on her back in the crib
- taking a warm bath with your baby

If it's their fussy time of day — usually late afternoon or evening — try the previous suggestions, and:
- reduce household needs, e.g., prepare supper ahead of time, have activities planned for other children
- have your partner, a family member, or some other person available to help out so you can be with your baby
- try holding the baby in different positions — some babies cry less when they are put to the shoulder and held upright

If you have tried all of these hints and your baby is still crying, remember that it is more important for you to stay calm than it is to stop the baby's crying. Crying will not hurt your baby. Shaking your baby is dangerous. If you are frustrated, put your baby in a safe place and leave the room for a few minutes.

Some parents are afraid that if they give too much attention, they will spoil their baby. This is not true. Babies need attention, cuddling, and handling. When babies cry, they need more care, not less. Crying is their way of telling you they need something. The best thing to do is to pick up and cuddle your baby.

What is colic?

There is no clear reason or prevention for colic. Infants who have colic tend to:
- have long periods of crying, fussiness, and restlessness throughout the day
- become more fussy in the late afternoon or early evening
- be difficult to soothe
- appear to be in pain

Colic can occur in breastfed or formula-fed infants. It usually begins at about two to three weeks of age and lasts until the third or fourth month. Colic usually stops quite suddenly.

Colic can be very disturbing to the whole family. It can be hard to stay calm while caring for a colicky baby. If you're stressed and frustrated by the baby's crying, and feel you might hurt the baby, put the baby in the crib and close the door. Take a break until you feel calmer or someone has come to help you.

Although there are no proven treatments, parents have found some things that may help with colic, for example:
- carrying your baby as much as possible
- having a regular routine of feeding, sleeping, and activity
- responding quickly to crying
- lowering the lights and noise in the room
- gentle movements and rhythmic rocking
- when your baby is fussy, don't over-handle her or pass her among a lot of people
- taking your baby for a car ride
- massaging your baby
- bathing your baby or taking your baby in the bath with you
- some parents have developed special ways to hold their babies that comfort them

Sometimes mothers who have lots of milk have babies who act colicky. If you think this might be you, breastfeed longer on the first breast before switching to the other breast. For example, if you give both breasts for a feeding, give one breast longer. If your baby takes just one breast, try giving the same breast at the next feeding.

Occasionally, changes in your diet when you are breastfeeding may help with colic symptoms. Try removing foods from your diet such as milk or other foods that you think may be causing the crying. Do this for a week to see if it makes a difference to your baby. If the crying decreases, avoid that food until your baby outgrows the colic. If you plan to remove a major food or a whole food group, talk with a registered dietitian first.

Some formula-fed babies may react to cow's milk-based formula. Talk about any formula changes with your health care practitioner.

Colic is not your fault, and anxious or tense parents do not cause it. A colicky baby can be very difficult to cope with on your own. Before the stress of the baby's crying becomes unbearable, ask for help. Trusted friends, relatives, and neighbours may be able to help for short periods of time.

If nothing helps, check with your health care practitioner to ensure your baby is well. Your public health nurse or the BC NurseLine (1-866-215-4700) can also suggest help.

Shaken Baby Syndrome

Shaken baby syndrome happens when a baby or small child is shaken hard. This shaking can cause serious injury to a baby's neck or cause brain damage, blindness, paralysis, mental retardation, and seizures. Some babies die from being shaken. No parent thinks that he will shake his baby and cause her harm. Crying is the number one reason that caregivers harm babies.

Never shake, hit, or throw your baby, ever. It only takes a moment to change your life — and your baby's life — forever.

If you feel angry or afraid that you may hurt your baby, put your baby down somewhere safe and call someone to help you right away. Do not try to care for your baby when you are angry. Call someone from your support team, your health care practitioner or the Crisis and Information Line listed under "Other Emergency Numbers" near the front of your local telephone book.

Only leave your baby with caregivers you can trust to control their anger. Tell them they must never shake your baby. If they are frustrated or cannot calm your baby, tell them to call you for help. If you know or think that someone has anger management problems, do not leave your baby with that person.

Never, ever shake your baby.

If you have a babysitter tell her she must never shake or hit your baby.

If you have shaken your baby, call your health care practitioner right away. Don't lay your baby down hoping that he will be better after a rest. Delaying medical help can cause more harm to your baby.

Do not shake your baby if he is choking or needs resuscitation. Shaking will only make him worse.

Anger Management

It can be very difficult to deal calmly with a crying baby day after day. Many parents feel they are responsible for the crying or that they are bad parents. Crying won't last forever and it is OK to ask for help.

Have a plan to help you stay calm and deal with the difficult times.

- If you are becoming angry, put your baby down and hold onto something you can't throw. Count to ten, leave the room, cry into or pound a pillow, or run on the spot. Don't touch your baby until you are calm.

- Ask someone to be your immediate back up, someone you can call if you are losing control. Keep their number close by your phone.

- Take regular breaks. Have someone take over so you can rest, walk, or just get away. Be sure the caregiver has a plan if the crying is hard to cope with.

- Talk with your partner about how you can help each other.

- Talk with other parents about how they coped.

- Talk with your health care practitioner about courses on anger management or parenting.

If you are concerned about your baby:

- If it's an emergency, call 911 or the local emergency number in your phone book.

- Check the BC HealthGuide handbook to learn about ways to manage over 190 health conditions and concerns. This includes when to see a doctor or other health professional.

- Visit BC HealthGuide OnLine and the BC HealthFiles at www.bchealthguide.org for more in-depth health information. These resources cover over 3,000 conditions and concerns. This includes when to see a doctor or other health professional.

- Call the BC NurseLine, at 1-866-215-4700, to speak to a registered nurse if you need:
  - more information
  - help to decide when it's best to see a health professional
  - help to decide when its safe to try home treatment

- Pharmacists are also available through the BC NurseLine between 5 p.m. and 9 a.m. every day.

- If you need a translator for this information, BC NurseLine can provide service in 130 languages.

- If your baby is under the care of a doctor, specialist, or other health care professional, always follow their advice. The BC HealthGuide handbook, online website, BC HealthFiles and the BC NurseLine **do not** replace the care provided by your doctor or other health care professional.

Baby Medical Care

Vitamin K Injection

The Canadian Pediatric Society advises that all newborns have an injection of vitamin K within six hours after birth. This injection helps prevent hemorrhagic disease of the newborn. Hemorrhagic disease of the newborn is a bleeding problem that occurs during the first few days of life. Babies are born with low levels of vitamin K, an important factor in blood clotting. In the newborn, the low level of vitamin K is the main cause of hemorrhagic disease.

If you do not want your baby to receive the injection, talk with your health care practitioner. Giving vitamin K by mouth may be an option. However, the recommended way to give vitamin K is by injection. Oral vitamin K needs to be given at birth and twice more over four to eight weeks.

Erythromycin Eye Ointment

The Canadian Pediatric Society recommends that all newborns receive treatment to prevent an infection of gonorrhea or chlamydia. These infections can get into the baby's eyes during birth. Today, an eye ointment is usually used to treat a baby's eyes. If not treated, these infections are severe and can cause blindness.

Treatment can be delayed for about one hour after birth. This allows for parent-infant contact, for the baby to be skin-to-skin with the mother, and for breastfeeding.

Universal Newborn Screening

Early Disease Screening
Even though your baby looks healthy in the first few days or even months of life, certain rare diseases can be present at birth. If untreated, these diseases can cause permanent mental retardation. Between 24 and 48 hours after birth,

every baby has a blood test. This is done by one heel prick that is sent for testing. If the test is positive, the baby's health care practitioner is told and more testing is planned. If further testing is positive, the baby will be given treatment. The sooner treatment is started, the better it will be for the baby.

Some diseases include:
- Hypothyroidism. This is treated by giving the baby a daily pill containing thyroid hormone.

- PKU (phenylketonuria), which is treated with a special diet.

- Galactosemia. This is treated with a special diet.

- Medium Chain Acyl-CoA Dehydrogenase Deficiency (MCAD). This is treated with a special diet.

Early Hearing Screening
New equipment is helping to screen hearing in younger and younger babies. If your hospital has this equipment and has begun this program, it will screen the hearing of your newborn and follow up with you as needed.

Hearing

Good hearing is very important for normal speech, language, and emotional development. Even mild or temporary hearing loss may result in delays in these areas of development. An audiologist can test your baby's hearing, even shortly after birth. About one out of every 300 babies will have some hearing loss at birth. Over half of babies with hearing loss are healthy and have no history of risk factors.

Some risk factors for hearing loss are:
- family history of permanent childhood hearing loss
- low birth weight or admission to the special care nursery
- jaundice that requires a transfusion

Points to Remember

If your baby doesn't get an early disease newborn screening (blood test) in the hospital, talk to your health care practitioner or public health nurse.

- exposure to some infections during pregnancy
- unusual eyes, nose, ears, mouth, or palate

The most common cause of hearing problems in very young children is ear infection (otitis media). Signs may include:
- irritability
- pain
- hand or fist to the ear
- fever
- mild hearing loss

Many factors can contribute to the risk of ear infection. Having cigarette smoke in the household will increase the risk of ear disease.

If you think your baby cannot hear, or if you have questions about screening, contact your health care practitioner or audiologist immediately. For more information related to hearing, see pages 137–138.

Vision

From birth, babies can distinguish light and dark, shapes, and patterns. When they are quiet and alert, babies can focus on objects 18 to 45 cm (7 to 18 in.) away for brief periods of time. Babies prefer to look at faces rather than objects, especially their mother's eyes.

It is not uncommon for your baby's eyes to "wander" or cross independently at times. This is normal in the first three months until he develops proper eye co-ordination. Constant eye wandering should not be ignored.

Some important points about your baby's vision:
- Children with a family history of a lazy or crossed eye are at a higher risk of having an eye problem.

- Early treatment of turned eye or decreased vision is very important for sight.

- If you have any concerns about your baby's vision, contact your health care practitioner.

Thrush (Yeast Infection)

Thrush is a common infection in infants. Thrush appears as a whitish-gray coating on the tongue and on the insides of the cheeks and gums. This coating is not easily wiped off. Babies may also develop thrush on their skin. Most babies do not have any pain or complications with thrush. For more information, see page 105. If you think your baby has thrush, see your health care practitioner.

Circumcision

Circumcision is surgery to remove the layer of skin (foreskin) that covers the head of the penis and part of the shaft. The Canadian Pediatric Society does not recommend routine circumcision because it is not medically necessary. However, some parents may choose this for religious reasons. There is pain during and after the procedure. Complications from circumcision include bleeding, infection, cutting the foreskin too short or too long, and poor healing. The cost of circumcision is not covered by provincial medical plans.

Allergies

Allergic symptoms in babies with food allergies may include:
- stomach pains
- diarrhea
- vomiting or frequent spitting up
- skin rashes or eczema
- constant runny nose

These symptoms may have other causes. If your baby frequently has any of these symptoms, talk them over with your health care practitioner or public health nurse. Ask for a referral to a registered dietitian, doctor, or nurse who specializes in allergies. If you are breastfeeding, you may need to change your own food choices.

Breastfeeding is the best way to prevent allergies to cow's milk and other foods. Babies from families with allergies are more likely to have allergies themselves. For these babies, avoid any exposure to cow's milk or cow's-milk formula. Do not introduce solids until six months of age.

Removing a major food or a whole food group requires careful planning with a registered dietitian in order to meet your nutritional needs. Ask your health care practitioner for more information on food allergies.

High Temperatures

Fever is usually caused by an infection. The source of the infection can be bacteria or a virus. Fever is the normal process of fighting an infection. It is important to watch your baby's behaviour. Often, this is more important than the actual degree on the thermometer. If you think your baby has a fever, take action right away. Babies less than six months old should be taken to their doctor if they have a fever. Call your health care practitioner or the BC NurseLine's 24-hour toll-free number, at 1-866-215-4700, if you are unsure.

Some signs of fever in your baby are:
- the back of the neck feels hot, even when extra clothing is removed
- having no interest in usual things
- looking ill or overly sleepy
- looking flushed or pale
- may be sweaty
- may be extra thirsty

What kind of thermometer should I use?
Use an easy-to-read thermometer, such as a digital one. A rectal thermometer is not recommended as this might cause rectal injuries. You might want to be prepared by buying a thermometer before your baby arrives.

How should I take the temperature?
If you suspect that your baby has a fever, you can check by taking a temperature under his armpit.

What is a normal temperature range?
Your baby's body temperature changes throughout the day. It is lowest in the early morning and highest in the early evening. Normal temperature taken under the armpit is 36.5°C to 37.4°C (97.7°F to 99.3°F). Your infant may have a higher or lower temperature and still be considered normal.

Taking your baby's temperature:
- Do not take your baby's temperature by mouth.

- Put the tip of the thermometer in the centre of the armpit.

- Tuck the arm snugly against the body, then comfort and distract your baby.

- After about one minute the thermometer will beep if it's digital. If it is not digital, wait about five minutes. Gently remove the thermometer and read the temperature.

- An armpit temperature is usually 0.3°C (0.5°F) to 0.6°C (1°F) lower than a reading taken from the mouth.

- If you find your baby has a temperature by taking it under the arm, check it again.

- Forehead strips or pacifier thermometers are not good ways to take a temperature.

When your baby has a fever, check the BC HealthGuide handbook and use the helpful tips to learn when to consult a health care practitioner and when to use home treatment.

Call the BC NurseLine for confidential health information and advice to learn how to assess and manage your baby's fever.

Acetylsalicylic acid (ASA or aspirin) should **not** be given to babies, children, or teenagers. If used when there is a fever, there is a link between ASA and the development of a very dangerous illness called Reye's Syndrome (see page 148).

Points to Remember

Immunizations may cause a temporary fever.

Points to Remember

Not every sick baby will have a fever, especially if they are less than one month old. Some signs of a sick baby may be poor feeding or not acting normally.

Contact your primary health care practitioner if **you** think your baby may be sick. You can also call the BC NurseLine at 1-866-215-4700.

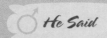
Baby Safety

Maintaining Basic Hygiene

During your pregnancy and after the birth of your baby, you can keep your family healthy by following these practices:

Washing hands — wash your hands with soap and water for 15 seconds before feeding your baby, after using the bathroom or handling diapers, handling pets, sneezing, or coughing. Make sure your older children do this as well.

Cleanliness — keep high chairs, bibs, and eating areas clean by washing with water and soap after each use. Clean and sanitize other surfaces in the home. It is important to clean the surfaces that your baby will come in contact with. These include floors, toys, teething ring, crib, stroller, changing table, etc. Hint: Use a bleach/water solution.

For additional information, see Food Safety on page 41 and Pet Safety on page 42.

General Home Safety Tips

You will have to protect your baby from all danger. Not surprisingly, most injuries can be prevented and happen in your own home:
- when you are not prepared for your baby's next stage of development, such as learning to roll over, crawl, or walk

- when you are busy with something else

- when either you or your baby are tired

Childproof your home *before* your baby begins moving around.
- Fasten carpet on stairs and remove loose rugs to avoid falling while carrying your baby.

- Post poison control, ambulance, and doctor's numbers and other emergency numbers near your phone so you can find them quickly.

- Install smoke detectors and a fire extinguisher. Plan an escape route to help you and your baby get out safely in case of fire. Check your smoke detector batteries. A helpful hint — check them each time you turn your clock forward in the spring and back in the fall.

- To prevent burns, keep the temperature in your hot water heater below 49°C (120°F).

- Remove leaded PVC mini-blinds that may be in your home. Do not have any dangling cords in or near the baby's crib or the floor.

- Know how to help a choking baby. Courses on basic first aid and baby and home safety may be available through community centres, St. John Ambulance, and the Red Cross. Check with your public health nurse for courses in your area.

- Furniture such as bookcases or television stands that could topple or fall during an earthquake should be fastened to the wall.

- See *Toddler's First Steps* for more information on childproofing your home (see Resources).

Keeping Your Baby Safe
- Toys should be soft, non-toxic, and washable. Toys that have no removable small parts or sharp edges are best.

- Keep small objects, such as pins (e.g., large diaper pins), coins, buttons, marbles, and disc batteries, out of reach and in safe containers.

- Keep all small objects out of the crib and out of reach.

- Never leave your baby alone with a toddler, a pet, a bottle, or on a soft surface.

- To prevent burns, never hold the baby while smoking, drinking a hot drink, cooking, or handling a hot utensil.

- Move baby's crib away from long mobiles, blinds, or curtain cords to avoid strangling.

- Always ask door-to-door canvassers and service personnel for ID. Public health nurses will call to make an appointment and should also be wearing identification.

Safe Baby Equipment

Playpens

Playpens must meet these guidelines:
- Playpen walls should be mosquito-type netting. Your little finger should not be able to pass through the mesh.

- Have no more than two wheels or casters.

- Have walls at least 48 cm (19 in.) high.

- All parts must be free from rough or sharp edges. Hinges should be designed to prevent pinching or unintended collapse.

- Any open holes drilled in metal, plastic, or wood components should be less than 3 mm (1/8 in.) or more than 10 mm (3/8 in.) in diameter.

- All parts that are small enough for a baby to choke on must be firmly attached.

- Vinyl rails and mattress pads should not be torn.

Do not leave your infant in a drop-sided mesh playpen unless all of the sides are fixed firmly in the fully raised position. Do not put scarves, necklaces, long cords, pillows, or large toys in a playpen. Many brands of playpens made in the 1990s have been recalled because they can injure or kill babies. Always check for recalls before accepting a second-hand playpen or portable crib.

Baby Walkers

Baby walkers are banned in Canada because they allow babies to move too fast and can cause serious head injuries. Instead, use an activity centre that doesn't move around on the floor.

Soothers

- Make sure the soother is a one-piece design.

- If your baby has thrush, replace or boil the soother for two minutes each day to prevent re-infecting your baby's mouth.

- Wash the soother with warm water. Be sure it is clean for your baby.

- Never wet the soother in your own mouth as this passes your mouth germs to your baby.

- Throw away any soother with an unusual colour or texture or if it becomes sticky, cracked, or torn.

- Check the soother often — give a strong tug on the nipple to make sure it won't come off the shield.

- Never use a cord to attach the soother to your baby.

- Never dip the soother into honey or any other sweetener. This causes tooth decay.

Do not give honey to babies less than 12 months of age. It can cause serious infection.

Strollers

- Use the five-point harness to prevent your baby from falling forward and tipping the stroller over.

- Be careful to prevent injury to fingers when folding and unfolding a stroller. Also be careful when changing the handle on reversible handle strollers.

- Do not hang your purse or heavy packages on the stroller handle. They can upset the stroller's balance.

- Check the stroller regularly for sharp edges, loose folding parts, brakes that don't work properly, and loose wheels.

- Always read the manufacturer's instructions for a new or used stroller.

Jogging or Running Strollers

Jogging strollers are meant for uneven surfaces such as paths, trails, or snow. Until your baby is at least one year old, do not jog with your baby in one of these strollers. Infants have weak neck muscles and cannot handle the constant jostling or the bumpy terrain when on trails. If used as a stroller for infants, they must have a fully reclining seat. Always use a five-point harness to secure your baby into these types of strollers. They are bulky and do not fold easily, so may not be the best choice if you plan to load a stroller in the back of your car.

Baby Carriers

Baby carriers can be soft strap-on carriers, slings, or framed back carriers.

Safety tips for slings or strap-on carriers:
- Always read the instructions first.

- Make sure it has a firm, padded head support that adjusts to the size of your baby.

- Check that the leg holes are wide enough for your baby to be comfortable but small enough that the baby can't slip through.

- Never use a carrier while skiing, jogging, biking, or in a car.

- Do not use a carrier when you are doing any activity, such as cooking, that could harm your baby.

- Give your baby plenty of time out of the carrier to move, crawl, and explore her environment.

Framed Back Carrier

- Do not use a framed back carrier until your baby can sit alone—about six months of age.

- Never leave your baby alone, even when it seems safe.

- The carrier should have a wide, solid base so it can't tip over. Never place the carrier on a table with your baby in it.

- If a seat has wire supports that snap on the back, make sure they are secure.

- Fasten straps and restraining buckles every time you use the seat. They should be adjusted to fit comfortably and to prevent your baby from turning in the seat.

Babies in back carriers should not be placed on tables, counters, or furniture. An active baby may lunge forward, tip the carrier, and fall to the floor. This can cause a head injury.

A framed back carrier is not a car seat and must never be used as one.

Infant/Child Car Seats

Use an infant/child car seat every time your child travels in a car. Car seats are required by law and must meet Canadian Motor Vehicle Safety Standards (CMVSS).

When buying a child car seat:
- Look for the CMVSS label. Do not buy a child seat in the United States — it will not have this label.

- Look for a child seat that is easy to use and fits in your vehicle. Try it in your vehicle before buying it. Be sure it is easy to use so you will use it correctly every time.

- Look for a child seat with at least two sets of shoulder harness strap slots to allow room for growth. Make sure they are easy to adjust.

It is recommended that you do not buy a second-hand child seat. If you do, the child seat should be inspected and checked for any possible recalls. Make sure a second-hand child seat meets CMVSS standards. Do not use a child seat that has been in a crash or has passed the expiration date stamped on the seat. If no expiration date is present, check with the child seat manufacturer and do not use a seat that is more than 10 years old.

If you want to rent a child seat, contact your local health office for the names of local rental/loaner programs. You can also call the toll-free Child Seat Information Line 1-877-247-5551 for a list of providers.

When using your child seat:
- **Never** place a rear-facing child seat in a vehicle seat equipped with an active air bag.

- A rear-facing seat is safest. Use a rear-facing seat for as long as possible, at least until one year of age.

- Follow the instructions in your vehicle's owner's manual and the instructions that come with your child seat. They contain important information for safe installation of the seat.

- If you are securing the child seat with your vehicle's lap belt, make sure it is long enough to go through the child seat's frame or over the seat according to the instructions.

- Some lap-shoulder belt systems will need a locking clip. This special H-shaped metal clip must be used to lock the lap and shoulder portion of a seat belt to keep the child seat in position. Refer to the owner's manual for your vehicle for specific information.

Infant Seats
- Infant seats are for infants from birth or 2.3 kilograms (5 pounds) up to 9 to10 kilograms (20 to 22 pounds).

- Infant seats must be used in the rear-facing position. Always follow the manufacturer's instructions for the seat and your vehicle when putting the seat in your car.

- The safest place for the infant seat is in the middle of the back seat.

If your baby has outgrown the infant seat and is still under one year of age, use a convertible seat in the rear-facing posiiton. Your baby has outgrown his infant seat if he weighs over 9 to 10 kilograms (20 to 22 pounds) or his head is within 2.5 centimetres (1 inch) of the top edge of the seat. Use the convertible rear-facing seat until your baby is at least one year old or exceeds the rear-facing weight limit of the seat. This will prevent severe head and spinal cord injuries in a crash.

Points to Remember

When you leave the car for any reason, take time to unbuckle the child seat and bring your baby with you. An infant should never be left alone in a vehicle! Never. Not for any length of time.

Convertible Rear-facing Seats

- A convertible seat should only be used when your baby has outgrown the infant seat, weighs over 9 to 10 kilograms (20 to 22 pounds), and is still under one year of age.

- A convertible seat with a five-point harness is recommended.

Correct Installation

- Place the child seat, rear-facing, in the back seat. Read and follow instructions that come with the child seat.

- Lower the carrying handle behind the infant seat.

- Maintain the correct reclining angle for the child seat. The back of the rear-facing seat should be tilted back to a maximum of 45 degrees so the baby's head and body lie back comfortably. If your baby's head falls forward, the seat is too upright.

- Secure the child seat with the Universal Anchorage System (UAS) or with the adult seat belt and, if necessary, use a locking clip.

- Check the ICBC website for more information www.icbc.com/Road_Safety/carseat_instal_moreeq.html#clip

Never place a rear-facing infant or child seat in the front seat if there is an active air bag.

Correct Harnessing

- Always check the manufacturer's instructions and your vehicle's owner's manual.

- Buckle your baby into the infant/child seat before every trip, no matter how short.

- When rear-facing, the harness straps should be at your baby's shoulders, or slightly below, to ensure a snug fit. Raise the harness straps to the next slots in the seat back when the infant's shoulders are level with or above the lower slots.

- Avoid the use of head huggers that were not manufactured with the child seat. A rolled receiving blanket or towel, one on either side of the baby's head and body will provide support. A rolled washcloth or diaper between the crotch and the crotch strap can prevent slouching.

- Place your baby in the seat and fasten the harness snugly. Only one finger should fit between the harness and the baby's collarbone.

- Avoid dressing your baby in heavy clothing or bunting bags. Dress your baby in clothes that have arms and legs. In cold weather, put blankets over your baby after he's been fastened in the seat.

- On each trip, check the harness tension and raise the chest clip to the level of your baby's underarms. The chest clip holds the harness straps in place on the shoulders.

- Double back all harness straps that pass through buckles to prevent them from slipping under tension.

- Be sure that anyone who will have your baby in their car is aware of the correct use of child seats.

- For small babies, use a child seat without a lap pad or shield as these may come into contact with the baby's face and neck.

Reproduced and adapted with permission from the Insurance Corporation of British Columbia

For more information on car seats, see www.canadian-health-network.ca/ and search for "car seats."

Special Circumstances

Preterm Babies

Preterm babies or preemies are those who are born before 37 weeks gestation. Preemies may have immature organ systems. Generally the younger your baby's age at birth, the more health problems she may have. If your baby is 36 weeks gestation at birth he may have very few, or no problems at all. On the other hand a baby born at 25 weeks gestation would be expected to need intensive care and monitoring. Birth weight is usually closely related to the length of the pregnancy.

Your preterm baby may need to be separated from you at birth if special care is required. Have your partner go with the baby to the nursery if possible. You should be able to visit your baby soon after the birth.

Preterm babies, like all babies, need to be touched, stroked, and talked to, even while inside the incubator or isolette. When your baby is well enough, you may be encouraged to have skin-to-skin contact. This is called *Kangaroo Care*. Your baby is unwrapped and placed on your chest where he can hear your heart beat, feel you breathing, and breastfeed. A warm blanket is placed on the baby. Research shows that babies who have lots of contact with their mothers grow faster than babies who don't.

Small babies may have problems with feeding. Often you will need to pump breast milk to give for feedings.

Preterm babies may have problems breathing while in an infant car seat. They may be more floppy and the chin may drop down on the chest blocking breathing. They need to be checked in their car seat before leaving the hospital. After a feeding, the baby will be place in his car seat and observed for about an hour. The baby will be observed longer if the drive home is more than an hour.

Low Weight Babies

About one-third of low birth weight babies (less than 2.5 kg or 5 1/2 lb.) are born at term (40 weeks gestation).

Low weight babies may have some of the complications seen in the preterm baby. As with the preterm baby, the low weight baby should be encouraged to have skin-to-skin contact or Kangaroo Care. This will keep the baby warm and encourage extra breastfeeding. You may need extra support with breastfeeding.

Once at home, it is important that your preterm or low weight baby be placed on her back for sleeping.

Twins, Triplets, or More

Multiple births can cause complications with your pregnancy, labour and birth. The babies can be delivered vaginally or by caesarean section. The type of delivery depends on the position of the babies in your uterus, their gestational age, and their health.

Multiples can be breastfed successfully. Feeding early and often will help you to have enough milk for all of your babies. Try different positions for holding your babies while breastfeeding. Parents of multiples need extra support and assistance with their infants. Do not be afraid to ask for help when you get home.

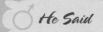

If you have any concerns about your baby's development or interaction with you, contact your health care practitioner to get advice.

Baby Development

Babies develop quickly because of rapid physical growth and brain development. This in turn helps a baby to develop thinking and language skills, and to grow socially and emotionally. Most babies develop in predictable ways and parents usually have a keen eye for what their baby is doing. Parents need to remember that each baby is unique.

While your baby is moving along on his or her own unique development timetable, you are a key partner in this development. Your caring, nurturing, and safe parenting will help ensure your baby's optimal development. Help your baby understand that his or her world is a safe and welcoming place.

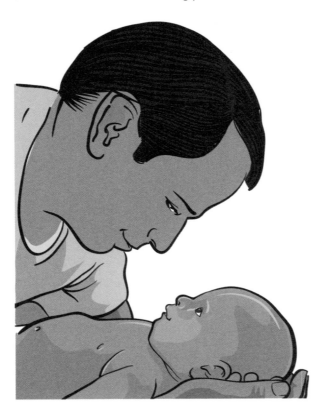

How can I be a caring and nurturing parent?

* Keep safe — always keep your baby warm, dry, comfortable, and safe.

* Keep healthy — ensure your baby's health through breastfeeding and good medical care.

* Follow cues — listen to and watch your baby. It is easy to over- or under-stimulate a baby. Follow their cues. If your baby turns her head away or fusses or cries, she wants to stop an activity.

* Give praise — when your baby accomplishes something new, give encouragement (clap, hug her, make happy noises, etc.).

* Be engaged — be there for your baby and always respond gently and soothingly.

* Discover your baby — your baby has a unique personality. Watch for this to emerge and celebrate your baby's uniqueness.

Physical Development

During the first six months your baby will gain about 240 grams (8 ounces) per week. Your baby will sleep about 15 hours per day in the first three to four months, and less time as she grows older. Eyesight and hearing develop and become more acute. Your baby's brain continues to develop.

First month:
- weight will drop after birth but will be regained quickly
- hand, arm, leg, and rooting movements are all reflex motions
- head flops if not supported
- focuses eyes at 18 to 45 cm
- stares at high contrast patterns and objects but does not reach
- recognizes mother's voice
- startles at noise

Second month:
- muscles relax and twitch less
- lifts head about 45 degrees while lying on tummy
- hands start to unfold
- may reach and grasp an object for a short time
- eyes move in unison and can track close moving objects
- may roll over one way

Third month:
- stretches out arms and legs
- rolls over from back to side
- holds head up to search for sounds and movement
- discovers feet and hands
- holds objects longer
- swipes with arms
- briefly bears weight on legs
- responds to detailed, high-contrast objects
- cuts first tooth (3rd to 6th month or later)

Fourth month:
- stands up and holds weight with help
- rolls over from front to side
- lifts head about 90 degrees
- sits with arms propped
- reaches for objects
- lets go of objects
- holds hands together

Fifth month:
- rolls over from front to back
- grabs toes and feet
- wiggles forward on floor
- reaches with a good aim
- transfers objects from hand to hand

Sixth month:
- holds head steady
- sits with back straight when propped
- grasps small objects and studies them
- rolls in both directions
- understands that object may be hiding behind another

Activities for Healthy Development

- Always supervise your baby to prevent falling.

- Baby proof your home so that everything harmful is out of the way.

- Hold the things you want your baby to see close to her eyes so she can focus clearly.

- Have lots of supervised tummy time on a mat so your baby can kick and move.

- Provide bright hanging objects that make noise within hitting range.

- Give clean rattles and toys that your baby can feel and mouth.

- Provide a variety of toys and objects with textures.

- Play in front of a mirror.

- Create safe play spaces on the floor.

- Take lots of walks with your baby in the fresh air.

- Give safe, clean, chewable toys.

- Everything will go in the mouth. Make sure objects are big enough that they cannot be swallowed.

- Extend bath time so your baby can kick and squeal while you supervise. **Never** leave your baby alone in the bath.

baby's physical development

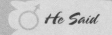 He Said

Our daughter put everything she could reach into her mouth. It got worse when she could move around more. I always gave her something safe to play with when I was changing her and made sure anything sharp or dangerous was a long way out of her reach.

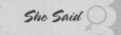

My mother-in-law kept saying I was spoiling our baby by carrying her all the time and picking her up when she fussed. But I had read about child development and knew just the opposite was true. Now our little girl is trusting and calm. She knows we will always be there for her, and that we come back if we've been away. I'm glad I listened to my own heart and did what I knew was right.

Social/Emotional Development

The first six months are an important time for you and your baby. Take time to give love, hugs, smiles, and lots of reassurance. Can you spoil a new baby? No. Research has shown that well-loved babies do better in every way. What about crying? Again, research says that you should go to and comfort a crying baby within one or two minutes.

First month:
- is alert 1 out of every 10 hours
- enjoys eye contact
- smiles at faces
- recognizes parents' voices
- begins to trust caregiver
- cries if under or over stimulated
- persistent crying can start at about two to three weeks

Second month:
- responsive smiling
- communicates moods
- enjoys visual stimulation
- studies faces
- your baby's personality becomes more obvious
- cries to have needs met
- persistent crying usually peaks in the second month

Third month:
- makes eye contact
- smiles at faces and may laugh out loud
- knows difference between parents and strangers
- stops crying when you come in the room
- persistent crying usually stops in month three or four

Fourth month:
- laughs hard when tickled
- greets caregiver
- starts social gestures
- may move arms to signal "pick me up"
- enjoys social interaction

Fifth month:
- turns head toward speaker
- watches your mouth movements
- shows interest in colours
- pushes away disliked actions

Sixth month:
- mimics facial expressions
- exhibits moods with varied sounds and body movements
- may be shy or afraid of strangers
- responds to her name
- raises arms to signal she wants to be picked up
- likes her reflection

Activities for Healthy Development
- Have skin-to-skin contact with newborns.

- Always respond to crying within one or two minutes.

- Look into your baby's eyes; you will fall in love.

- Talk to your baby soothingly.

- Don't feel rejected if your baby turns away from you — young babies get tired easily.

- Plan daily quiet times with your baby.

- Don't jiggle crying babies — use slow, gentle motions.

- Don't over stimulate your baby.

- Copy your baby's movements and sounds.

- Rock and cuddle your baby.

- Do finger and toe playing.

Language Development

Babies first communicate by crying. Then they learn to make sounds and smile. This is "talking." Eventually they learn to use words. Communicating is a two-way street—so talk to your baby when your baby "talks" to you. Your baby will want to "talk" with you using her language.

First month:
- responds to voices
- small cooing begins
- responds when you talk
- communicates with smiles, gazes, and crying

Second month:
- discovers her own voice
- gurgles, coos, and squeals
- exhibits emotions
- smiles at mother or father when they smile
- looks at mother's or father's face when they talk

Third month:
- begins extended vowel sounds, e.g. "ah"
- starts to laugh
- has different cries for different needs

Fourth month:
- changes shape of mouth to change sounds
- sputters, gurgles
- begins babbling
- laughs out loud

Fifth month:
- babbles ("ba-ba")
- tries to mimic sounds
- squeals and is interested in the sounds the parent makes

Sixth month:
- longer and more varied sounds ("ga-ga dada, papa")
- experiments with different volumes and pitches of sounds
- squeals with delight when happy
- makes sputtering sounds with the lips and tongue
- makes sounds or talks to toys

Activities for Healthy Development

- Talk to your baby using the language in which you feel most comfortable. Don't worry if it is not English.

- Comfort your crying baby with a soothing voice and gentle words.

- Hum to your child.

- Sing nursery rhymes and songs.

- Read and tell stories to your baby, even your newborn.

- Play games (peek-a-boo, imitating sounds your baby makes, gentle tickling, shaking toys, etc.).

- Talk to your baby about what you are doing (bathing, diapering, nursing, etc.).

- Call your baby by name.

- Make sure your baby can see your face when you talk to him.

- Talk to your baby about what you think he is trying to tell you with his coos, cries, and babbles.

- Mimic any sounds your baby makes. This encourages your baby to make more sounds.

baby's
language
development

If you have any concerns about your baby's development or interaction with you, contact your health care practitioner to get advice.

When should you be concerned about your baby's development?

If your baby:

- has an unusually stiff or floppy body
- is not watching faces by two to three months
- is unusually quiet or placid
- has unusual difficulties with feeding
- does not startle to loud noises
- holds hands in tight fists
- does not follow activities with his eyes
- does not seem to recognize his mother
- does not vocalize
- does not seek sounds with his eyes
- is persistently unable to settle

For more information on your child's development after six months, refer to *Toddler's First Steps*. A copy of this publication is available to all BC parents of children aged six months to three years by contacting your local public health office. For other helpful information on a variety of topics related to infant and child development and parenting, see the *Child Development Series* in the BC HealthFiles found at www.bchealthguide.org.

Notes

_____

_____

_____

_____

_____

_____

_____

_____

_____

_____

_____

_____

_____

_____

_____

_____

_____

_____

Parents' Best Chance

The last word in this handbook is to you, as a parent. You have wonderful opportunities to care for and nurture your baby, and help your baby become happy and healthy. While you read the words of other parents, think about the kind of parent you would like to be.

Here are a few thoughts from other parents on how they want to parent.

I want to be a parent who:
- is there whenever my baby needs me
- feeds my baby whenever and wherever she is hungry
- keeps my baby safe
- keeps my baby as healthy as possible
- plays with my baby every chance I get
- helps my baby explore the world
- listens to my baby
- reads and sings to my baby
- knows when to walk away and cool down
- knows when to seek advice and help
- makes time to look after my own health

To Do

Talk over your parenting dreams with your partner and together write down a few goals you can use to guide your parenting.

To Do

Take a few moments to rethink your support team and decide whom you might want to add.

Health Care Support

_____

_____

Personal Support

_____

_____

_____

A New Support Team

A support team is one of the most important resources you can have. It can help you be the parent you want to be. Throughout this handbook you have explored the ways support teams can help during and after pregnancy. Once you leave pregnancy behind and start to care for and nurture your baby, you will find that you need new members on your medical and personal support team.

Resources

Alcohol and Drug Information

All provinces and territories have programs for people with alcohol and other drug problems. Ask your health care practitioner or check in the yellow pages under "Alcohol" or "Drug" information.

Residents of British Columbia can call the Ministry of Health's Alcohol and Drug Referral Service. It is a confidential, information line to alcohol and other drug programs in the province.
Phone: toll-free 1-800-663-1441

For information on breastfeeding and alcohol, visit the Motherisk website, or call its Alcohol and Substance Use Helpline.
Phone: 1-877-327-4636
Website: www.Motherisk.org

BC College of Family Physicians

#350 1665 West Broadway
Vancouver, BC V6J 1X1
Phone: 604-736-1877
Fax: 604-736-4675
Website: www.bccfp.bc.ca

BC College of Midwives

College Of Midwives Of British Columbia
Suite 210 1682 West 7th Avenue
Vancouver, BC V6J 4S6
Phone: 604-742-2230
Fax: 604-730-8908
Website: www.cmbc.bc.ca

BC Dental Association

Suite 400 1765 West 8th Avenue
Vancouver, BC V6J 5C6
Phone: 604-736-7202 or 1-888-396-9888
Fax: 604-736-7588
Email address: post@bcdental.org
Website: www.adsbc.bc.ca

BC Dental Hygienists' Association

Suite 311 9600 Cameron Street
Burnaby, BC, V3J 7N3
Phone: 604-415-4559
or toll-free for members in BC: 1-888-305-3338
Fax: 604-415-4579
Email: info@bcdha.bc.ca
Website: www.bcdha.bc.ca

BC HealthGuide Program

The BC HealthGuide Program has four components:
- The *BC HealthGuide* handbook. It is available in English and French, and as the *First Nations Health Handbook*. To request your copy, call 1-800-465-4911.

- BC HealthGuide OnLine. This reliable website with in-depth health information is found at www.bchealthguide.org

- The BC HealthFiles is a series of easy-to-read one-page Fact Sheets on a variety of environmental, public health, and safety topics. These may be of interest to you and your family. They can be found on BC HealthGuide at www.bchealthguide.org

- The BC NurseLine. This confidential telephone nursing service is available 24 hours a day, seven days a week. It includes the BC NurseLine Pharmacist Service for medication inquiries. The pharmacist service is available between the hours of 5 p.m. and 9 a.m. daily. Both services answer your health care questions and concerns, including when to see a doctor or visit emergency.

Phone: 604-215-4700 (in the Lower Mainland)
or toll-free elsewhere in BC: 1-866-215-4700
Deaf and Hearing Impaired: 1-889-215-4700
Translation services are available in over 130 languages.

Breastfeeding

La Leche League
Website: www.lalecheleague.org

Registered Nurses Association of British Columbia, Policy
Statement: *Breastfeeding: Protection, Promotion and Support*:
Website: www.rnabc.ca/registrants/publications_and_
resources/topic_policy_statements.htm

For information on formula feeding your baby,
refer to HealthFile # 68l.
Website: www.bchealthguide.org/healthfiles

Canadian Health Network

Website: www.canadian-health-network.ca

Canadian Pediatric Society

Website: www.cps.ca

Canadian Red Cross

The Canadian Red Cross offers a ChildSafe Program that
teaches CPR and basic skills for dealing with emergencies.
Look in the white pages for your local branch.
Phone: toll-free 1-888-307-7997
Website: www.redcross.ca

Children with Disabilities

Your public health nurse can help if you think your baby has
a developmental problem or a disability. Most communities
have an Infant Development Program for children. Staff in
this program can help you with activities for your baby that
will encourage development. You will also have help finding
other support services.

Check BC HealthGuide for helpful information that includes
access to the database of the National Organization for Rare
Disorders (NORD).
Website: www.bchealthguide.org

Child Care

Your local Ministry of Children and Family Development
office or health office can give you information to help you
select a child care facility.

See BC HealthGuide and the Canadian Health Network for
more tips and information on choosing child care providers.
Website: www.bchealthguide.org
Website: www.canadian-health-network.ca

Dial-a-Dietitian

For nutrition information for you and your baby.
Phone: 604-732-9191(Lower Mainland)
or toll-free 1-800-667-DIET (3438)
Website: www.dialadietitian.org

Family Planning

Planned Parenthood Federation of Canada
Website: www.ppfc.ca

Sexuality and U
Website: www.sexualityandu.ca

Options for Sexual Health Facts of Life Line
A confidential phone line staffed by registered nurses and
trained volunteers.
Phone: 604-731-7803 (in the Lower Mainland)
or toll-free 1-800-739-7367
Website: www.factsoflifeline.com

Family Violence

When violence happens, get help. If it is an emergency,
call 911 or the operator and ask for the police.

Crisis lines and transition houses in your community are
listed under the Emergency tab found in the first portion of
the TELUS (BCTel) phone book. (Note: In Vancouver, this
information appears inside the front cover page.)

You can get also information on the victim services closest
to you by calling the VictimLink phone line. The line
operates 24 hours a day, 7 days a week.
Phone: toll-free 1-800-563-0808
Access for hearing impaired: 604-875-0885

Pride Line: 7 days a week, 7 a.m. – 10 p.m.
Phone: 604-684-6869 (Lower Mainland)
or toll-free 1-800-566-1170 (outside Lower Mainland)

Fathering

Canadian Father Involvement Initiative
Website: www.cfii.ca

Dads Can
Website: www.dadscan.org

Ask Dr. Sears
Website:www.askdrsears.com

Immunization Information

For information on immunizations, visit:
Canadian Pediatric Society
Website: www.cps.ca

BC HealthFiles
Website: www.bchealthguide.org/healthfiles

BC HealthGuideOnline
Website: www.bchealthguide.org

Or call your public health office or the BC NurseLine
Phone: 1-866-215-4700

Insurance Corporation of British Columbia (ICBC)

For information on safe child restraints.
Public Affairs and Corporate Marketing, ICBC
240 151 West Esplanade
North Vancouver, BC V7M 3H9
Website: www.icbc.com

Legal Paperwork

Employment Standards
Website: www.labour.gov.bc.ca/esb/esaguide/

Forms for Birth Certificate and Registration of Birth
Website: www.vs.gov.bc.ca/forms

PharmaCare Coverage
Phone: 604-683-7151 (Lower Mainland)
or toll-free 1-800-663-7100 (outside Lower Mainland)
Website: www.healthservices.gov.bc.ca/pharme/

Motherisk

Provides specific support for pregnant and breastfeeding women. Motherisk call centre is open Monday to Friday from 9 a.m. to 5 p.m., Eastern Standard Time.
Phone: 416-813-6780
Website: www.motherisk.org

Motherisk Alcohol and Substance Use Helpline
Phone: toll-free at 1-877-327-4636.

Motherisk Nausea and Vomiting of Pregnancy Helpline
Phone: toll-free at 1-800-436-8477

Motherisk HIV Helpline
Phone: toll-free at 1-888-246-5840.

Multiple Births

Multiple Births Canada
Website: www.multiplebirthscanada.org

Talk with the staff in your local hospital or your public health office for information on twins and triplets associations and support groups in your area.

Postpartum Depression

For information about postpartum depression support groups, contact your public health nurse.

The Pacific Post Partum Support Society has a guide for mothers who have postpartum depression: *Post Partum Depression and Anxiety: A Self Help Guide for Mothers*.
104 1416 Commercial Drive
Vancouver, BC V5L 3X9
Phone: 604-255-7999
Website: www.postpartum.org

The BC Reproductive Mental Health Program provides counselling to women with depression in pregnancy and postpartum. They have information and resources on their websites.
Websites: www.bcrmh.com and www.bcwomens.ca

Safe Start

Safe start is an injury prevention program of BC Children's Hospital. It provides information to parents and caregivers on how to make homes and cars safer.
Phone: 604-875-3273 (Lower Mainland)
or toll-free 1-888-331-8100 (outside Lower Mainland)
Website: www.cw.bc.ca/safestart

Sexually Transmitted Infections

Motherisk offers information and counselling to Canadians about HIV and other STIs (see Motherisk).

Smoking Information

BC Smokers Helpline
Phone: toll-free 1-877-455-2233
Website: www.quitnow.ca

Health Canada
Website: www.hc-sc.gc.ca/hecs-sesc/tobacco/quitting/

BC Stop Smoking Project
Website: www.bc.lung.ca

BC HealthGuide OnLine
Website: www.bchealthguide.org

Society of Obstetricians and Gynecologists of Canada

780 Echo Drive
Ottawa, ON K1S 5R7
Phone: 613-730-4192 or toll-free 1-800-561-2416
Fax: 613-730-4314
Website: www.sogc.org

Support for Parents

Support programs, Pregnancy Outreach Programs (POP), and family resource centres offer programs and services to support families and single parents. Contact your local health office or public health nurse for more information.

Pregnancy Outreach Programs
Website: www.bcapop.ca

For advice on financial support, including BC's Family Bonus or family maintenance, contact the Ministry of Human Resources. For information about enforcement of maintenance orders, contact the Ministry of Attorney General. Check the blue pages of your phone book for the nearest office.

Support groups, such as Parents without Partners, Mother Goose! and Nobody's Perfect, and the family resource program (Family Place) are in many communities. Contact your local public health office, mental health agency, or Ministry of Human Resources office about programs.

Nobody's Perfect Parenting Program,
BC Council for Families
Phone: 604-738-0568

If you plan to return to school, the Ministry of Human Resources may be able to help you look at options for your education and planning your career.

St. John Ambulance

St John Ambulance offers programs in first aid, CPR, and child care. Local branches of St. John Ambulance are listed in the white pages of your telephone directory, and in the Yellow Pages under "First Aid Services."
Phone: 604-321-2651
Website: www.sja.ca

Toddler's First Steps

Contains information about child care and development from the ages of six months to three years old. Available from your local public health office or the BC Ministry of Health website.
Website: www.health.gov.bc.ca/cpa/publications/firststeps.pdf

Glossary

abdomen
The front part of the body between the chest and the pelvis.

acetaminophen
A medicine that is used to relieve pain and decrease fever.

acetylsalicylic acid (ASA)
Commonly known as aspirin. A drug used to relieve pain and reduce fever. Do not give aspirin (ASA) to babies, children, or teenagers because there is an association between the development of Reye's Syndrome and the use of aspirin.

AIDS
Acquired Immune Deficiency Syndrome. It can develop if one becomes infected by the HIV virus.

amniocentesis
A diagnostic test for finding genetic fetal abnormalities such as Down Syndrome. It is usually done between 15 to 18 weeks of pregnancy. It is done by removing a small amount of amniotic fluid using a needle under ultrasound guidance.

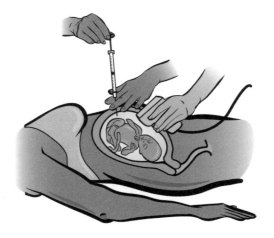

amniotic fluid
The liquid that surrounds the fetus. It helps the baby by absorbing bumps from the outside, maintaining an even temperature inside, and allowing the baby to move easily. When the amniotic sack ruptures at birth, it is often called the *water breaking*.

amniotic sac
The membrane inside the uterus that holds the fetus and amniotic fluid. (See diagram on page 149.)

antibiotic
Drugs used to fight many infections caused by bacteria. Antibiotics do not work against viral infections.

antihistamine
A drug that acts to relieve the effects of histamine, a normal body chemical that is thought to cause symptoms in people who are very sensitive to various allergens (substances causing a person to become sensitive).

Apgar test
A simple and easy way to measure how healthy a baby is. The test rates five areas: the baby's heart rate, breathing, muscle tone, reflexes, and skin colour. The rating is a number out of a total of 10 called the Apgar score. Most babies score an Apgar between 7 and 10.

Baby-Friendly Initiative
A global program of the World Health Organization (WHO) and UNICEF to encourage practices in hospitals and communities that promote, protect, and support breastfeeding.

bacterial vaginosis
A sexually transmitted disease of the vagina that can be cured. Caused by bacteria.

bilirubin
The yellow-coloured substance formed when the extra red blood cells break down after birth. Eliminated from the baby's body in its bowel movements. It is the cause of jaundice.

Braxton Hicks contractions
Contractions of the uterus that occur during pregnancy. They are not usually painful and can last for about a minute. Often called *practicing contractions*.

breech position
The unborn baby's buttocks, buttocks and legs, or legs are facing down and would be born first.

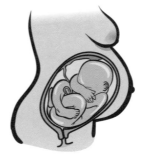

caesarean
A surgical procedure used to deliver a baby through incisions in the abdomen and the uterus. Often referred to as a caesarean birth or C-section.

cervix
The lower part of the uterus that protrudes into the vagina through which the baby passes during birth. (See diagram on page 149.)

chloasma
The darkening of the skin around the eyes and over the nose and cheeks during pregnancy. Often called the *mask of pregnancy.*

chorionic villus sampling (CVS)
A diagnostic test used to detect genetic abnormalities in the fetus. Done by removing a small amount of chorionic villi tissue through the woman's vagina or the abdomen. The test is unable to detect neural tube defects.

chromosome abnormality
Genetic defects in the structure of a baby's chromosomes.

circumcision
The surgical procedure to remove the layer of skin (foreskin) that covers the head of the penis and part of the shaft.

colic
Excessive and inconsolable crying in a normally developing infant.

colostrum
The first breast milk produced. It begins to be produced during pregnancy and is important for the baby's first feedings.

cue-based feeding
Feeding an infant when she shows an interest in feeding before reaching the crying state. Feeding cues include: rapid eye movements (eyes moving under eyelids), waking, stretching, stirring, hand-to-mouth movements, sucking, licking, and rooting.

dehydration
Loss of water from the body. Usually due to not taking in enough fluids. Can be serious.

diabetes
A disease that occurs when the body has difficulty making or using insulin (a hormone that makes it possible for the body to use sugar as a source of energy). Without the help of insulin, the blood sugar level will become much higher than normal.

dilation
The opening of the cervix during the first stage of labour. It is measured in centimetres and is about 10 centimetres when fully opened.

doula
A labour companion who is trained and experienced in childbirth, and provides continuous physical and emotional support during labour, birth, and the immediate postpartum period.

Down syndrome
A genetic disorder that causes physical abnormalities and mental disabilities.

ectopic pregnancy
A pregnancy in which the fertilized egg begins to develop outside the uterus.

eczema
A skin rash that often has itching, swelling, blistering, oozing, and scaling of the skin.

effacement
The ongoing thinning and shortening of the cervix during the first stage of labour.

embryo
The developing baby from the fourth week after the egg has been fertilized until the eighth week of pregnancy.

engorgement
Occurs when the breasts become overly full (swollen), hard, and painful. It is prevented by early (soon after birth) and frequent breastfeeding, not restricting the time for feeding, and ensuring the baby is welll latched on and feeding well.

Entonox
The drug nitrous oxide, commonly known as laughing gas. It is used to relieve pain during labour.

epidural
Local anaesthetic given into the space around the spinal cord, providing pain relief from the waist down. Used during labour and vaginal birth by some women and for most caesarean births.

episiotomy
An incision (cut) made in the area between the vagina and rectum to enlarge the space for the baby to pass through the vaginal opening.

erythromycin eye ointment
An antibiotic cream used in the eyes of newborns to prevent infection.

family-centred care
The process of providing safe, skilled care to meet the physical, emotional, and psychosocial needs of each mother, newborn, and family. Pregnancy and birth are considered to be a normal and healthy life event. Also recognizes the importance of family support and participation and care is adapted to meet their needs.

feeding on demand
Feeding a baby on cue when they indicate hunger by watching for the baby's feeding cues. Newborns feed frequently. This is the preferred approach. A regular timed schedule is not followed.

fetal
The unborn baby or fetus.

Fetal Alcohol Spectrum Disorder (FASD)
The full range of birth defects and disabilities that can result from with drinking alcohol during pregnancy. Can range from mild to very severe defects and developmental delays. Is totally preventable by not drinking during pregnancy.

fetus
The unborn baby from eight weeks until birth.
Also spelled *foetus*.

folic acid
One of the B vitamins that women of childbearing age (18 – 45 years old) are recommended to take before pregnancy and in early pregnancy to prevent defects of the spinal cord, such as spina bifida.

forceps
Spoon-like instruments that are placed on either side of the baby's head during some deliveries. They are used to gently help pull the baby out.

fundus
The top part of the uterus.

galactosemia
One of the disorders included in the Newborn Screening Test. A baby with this disorder cannot process galactose, a sugar found in milk. This is treated with a special diet.

gestational diabetes
Diabetes that can develop during pregnancy and usually disappears after birth. Women with gestational diabetes are at increased risk for developing diabetes in later life.

glucose screening (glucose tolerance test)
Screening test used to screen for gestational diabetes. Measures the mother's blood after drinking a liquid high in sugar.

groin
The place where the abdomen and the thigh meet.

group B streptococcus (group B strep)
Bacteria that is found in the vagina and bowel of 15 – 20% of healthy pregnant women. It can pass from the mother to the baby during birth and cause serious infection. Treated by antibiotics.

hemorrhagic disease
A bleeding problem that can occur during the first few days of life. Vitamin K is given to newborns to prevent hemorrhagic disease.

hemorrhoids
Painful, itchy, and sometimes bleeding veins that bulge out around your anus, especially during pregnancy or after birth.

HIV (Human Immunodeficiency Virus)
The virus that causes AIDS (Acquired Immune Deficiency Syndrome). Can be passed from the mother to the unborn child. Antiviral drugs are used to help prevent infant infection.

HSV (herpes simplex virus)
Common viral sexually transmitted disease.

hypertension
High blood pressure.

hypothyroidism
One of the disorders included in the Newborn Screening Test. A baby born with this disorder cannot make enough thyroid hormone. Thyroid hormone keeps a baby's body growing strong and healthy. Treated by giving a pill of thyroid hormone each day.

incontinence
Leakage of urine.

intravenous (IV)
Giving fluid through a vein.

jaundice
The breaking down of extra red blood cells, forming a yellow substance called bilirubin. When extra bilirubin accumulates, it appears in the skin, the mucous membranes, or the whites of the eyes. Common in newborns.

Kangaroo Care
Care that places a baby, even preterm babies, skin-to-skin with a parent. Babies benefit from the smell, sound of the heartbeat, and the warmth the parent provides. Improves the growth of preterm infants and gives parents an opportunity to be close to their baby.

Kegel exercises
Exercises to strengthen the vaginal and perineal area (between the vagina and anus).

labia
The fold of skin, on both sides, at the opening of the vagina in females. (See diagram on page 149.)

labour nurse
Registered nurse who provides nursing care to the pregnant mother and supports the family during labour and birth.

lactation consultant
A healthcare provider who has training and is certified to help women with breastfeeding. This person receives a certificate from the international board of lactation consultants.

lanugo
Fine hair that covers the body of the fetus.

let-down reflex
Hormonal reaction to the baby sucking on the breast that causes milk to flow into the breasts. May be felt as a warm, tingling feeling.

leukemia
Cancer of the tissues in the bone marrow, spleen, and lymph nodes.

linea nigra
A dark line between the pubic bone and the navel that appears in some women. Due to hormonal changes during pregnancy.

lochia
Bloody discharge flowing from the uterus and vagina following birth.

lymphoma
A tumor or condition affecting the lymph tissue.

mastitis
An infection of the breast tissue and/or milk ducts. There is always a hard, swollen, red, painful area in the breast.

maternal serum screening
Blood test offered to pregnant women to screen whether they are at an increased risk of carrying a baby with either Down syndrome or an open neural tube defect (spina bifida).

meconium
The baby's first bowel movement. It is a sticky, greenish-black substance present in the baby's intestine before birth. It is passed for one to two days after birth.

Medium Chain Acyl-CoA Dehydrogenase Deficiency (MCAD)
One of the disorders included in the Newborn Screening Test. A baby with MCAD may have problems using fats stored in their body for energy. The baby is healthy when eating well. This is treated with a special diet and not fasting.

menstruation
A woman's monthly bleeding. It is also called menses, menstrual period, or period.

milia
Small white raised spots commonly seen on a newborn's face. Milia are caused by plugged oil glands and usually clear within three to four weeks.

morning sickness
Nausea and vomiting that woman may experience during pregnancy. Commonly seen in the first trimester but can occur throughout the pregnancy.

non-stress test
Electronic monitoring test used before labour to check the functioning of the fetus' heart rate patterns in response to fetal movement.

otitis media
Infection of the middle ear. Most commonly seen in young children. It frequently follows or occurs at the same time as an upper respiratory infection (cold).

oxytocin
A hormone naturally produced by the body that is responsible for starting uterine contractions.

perinatal nurse
A Registered Nurse who provides nursing care for the woman, newborn, and the family during labour, birth, and postpartum.

perineum
The area between the vagina and the anus, including the pelvic floor muscles, the external genitals, urethra, and anus. (See diagram on page 149.)

Phenylketonuria (PKU)
One of the disorders included in the Newborn Screening Test. A baby with PKU is missing an enzyme that is needed to process the essential amino acid phenylalanine. It is found in certain foods. This is treated with a special diet.

pica
An unusual craving or compulsion to eat non-food substances. Examples of common substances craved for in pregnancy are dirt, clay, and laundry starch.

placenta
The structure that grows on the wall of the uterus during pregnancy that connects the fetus to the mother. Blood passes through the placenta to the baby, providing oxygen, nutrition, and antibodies. Blood circulated back to the mother's body brings waste from the baby's body for removal. The placenta also produces a number of hormones that affect the body during pregnancy. (See diagram on page 149.)

placenta previa
A condition in which the placenta covers all or part of the cervix. It can cause bleeding.

plaque
A sticky film of bacteria that is present in the mouth all the time. This bacteria is the primary cause of inflammation of the gums (gum disease or gingivitis) and tooth decay.

positional plagiocephaly
The flattening of one side or the back of the baby's head. It is caused by the baby always lying in the same position.

posterior position
The back of the unborn baby's head is toward the mother's back.

postpartum
The period after childbirth.

postpartum blues
Occur within the first 3–5 days after birth. Up to 80% of mothers can experience temporary emotional distress (from happiness to sadness). In most women these resolve without treatment within a week or two. Also known as the "baby blues."

postpartum depression
A variety of emotional problems that can affect the mother after giving birth. It is described as a group of symptoms that can change a woman's mood, behaviour, and outlook.

pregnancy gingivitis
Red, swollen, tender, and bleeding gums. Pregnancy gingivitis is caused by hormonal changes in pregnancy combined with poor oral hygiene. It can be prevented with correct gum care. If the condition persists, or there is extreme swelling, see a dentist or dental hygienist.

pregnancy-induced hypertension (PIH)
High blood pressure that occurs in pregnancy in a woman who has had normal blood pressure. High blood pressure disappears quickly after birth.

pre-labour
The time before labour actively begins when the uterus may start gentle but irregular contractions (Braxton Hicks).

prenatal
Related to the time from when a woman becomes pregnant to the time of birth.

prenatal supplement
Vitamin and/or mineral pill designed for pregnancy and taken in addition to a healthy diet. These supplements provide extra vitamins and minerals needed to help meet the needs of a growing baby.

public health nurse
Registered Nurse who provides prevention and health promotion services to mothers, infants and families in homes, preschools, schools, and other community settings.

pudendal block
Local freezing given around the vagina. This stops the pain in the vagina, vulva, and perineum. Given at the time of birth.

quickening
The first time a baby's movements can be felt by the pregnant woman.

Registered Midwife
A trained professional who provides care for women during normal pregnancy labour, birth, and after the baby is born.

Reye's syndrome
A serious disease that affects the organs of the body. It can cause very serious damage to the liver and the brain. Because there is an association between the development of Reye's Syndrome and the use of aspirin (ASA), babies, children, and teenagers should not be given aspirin (ASA).

Rh-negative
Women who are Rh-negative can develop antibodies to an Rh-positive baby. If there is mixing between the blood of the mother and baby, the woman's body may respond by developing antibodies as if it is allergic to the baby. This can be very serious for the baby. This is preventable. An injection or Rh immunoglobulin (RhIg) is given at about 28 weeks pregnancy. It will also be given at any time in pregnancy there is bleeding or an amniocentesis. Rh-negative women will also be tested after birth to determine if another injection of RhIg is needed.

rubella antibody screen
A blood test to determine a woman's immunity to rubella (German measles). If a woman becomes infected during pregnancy her unborn baby can be affected.

salmonella
A bacterium of the genus *Salmonella,* especially of a species causing food poisoning.

scrotum
The skin-covered pouch below the penis that contains the testes in males.

sexually transmitted infections (STIs)
Once called venereal diseases, these are spread mostly by sexual contact. There are about 20 identified types, including herpes, Hepatitis B, Chlamydia, AIDS/HIV, genital warts, gonorrhea, and syphilis. They can cause sterility, miscarriage, ectopic pregnancies, etc., and can affect the baby while in the uterus or at the time of birth. Treatment and prevention is available for most STIs.

shaken baby syndrome (SBS)
Shaken baby syndrome is a form of non-accidental head injury with or without impact, that results from violent shaking. It is a form of child abuse and can cause serious lifelong injuries or death.

show
Blood-tinged vaginal discharge that may be one of the signs of labour. Bloody show continues as labour progresses. It has blood in it because small blood vessels in the cervix break as the cervix thins and opens.

skin-to-skin
The naked or diaper-clad baby is placed on the mother's or partner's bare chest. A blanket is placed over both for warmth. Babies benefit from the smell, sound of the heartbeat, and the warmth of the parent's body. It also encourages breastfeeding.

station
The position of the baby's presenting part (the lowest part, usually the head) in relation to the mother's pelvic bones.

stillbirth
When a baby that appeared to be well during pregnancy is born dead.

stool
The waste that comes out of the bowels.

Sudden Infant Death Syndrome (SIDS)

The sudden and unexpected death of a healthy baby that remains unexplained after all known and possible causes have been carefully ruled out. Research suggests that cigarette smoke and the baby sleeping on its tummy are contributing factors. Also known as crib death.

supplements

Vitamin and/or mineral pill, taken in addition to a healthy diet. Supplements provide extra vitamins and minerals needed to help meet the needs of a growing baby.

surfactant

A substance formed in the lungs late in fetal life that helps to keep the small air sacs expanded. Infants born preterm without adequate amounts have difficulty breathing.

transcutaneous electronic nerve stimulation (TENS)

A method for relief of back pain. Electrodes are placed on the lower back. They are attached to a small, hand-held battery device. The stimulation gives tingling, buzzing, or prickling sensations over the back.

thrush

A yeast infection that can cause breast infection. Yeast grows well on milk and in warm moist areas (such as mother's nipples, infant's mouth, diaper area, and vaginal area). Generally responds well to treatment. Mother and baby are usually treated together. Continue to breastfeed.

toxoplasmosis

A disease caused by a parasite and transmitted by: eating raw or undercooked meat or other raw foods including fruits and vegetables; drinking unpasteurized milk; cleaning cat litter boxes; or working in gardens or playing in sandboxes that contain cat feces (poop). Can result in miscarriage, poor fetal growth, preterm birth, or stillbirth.

Babies born with toxoplasmosis may have serious physical and mental disabilities.

trimester

The nine months of pregnancy divided into three parts.

ultrasound test

A scan that uses very high-frequency sound waves (can't be heard by humans) to show the development of the baby in the uterus.

umbilical cord

Links the placenta to the baby. Nutrients and waste products pass through the umbilical cord. It is attached to the baby at the belly button. The umbilical cord is usually about 56 cm (22 inches) long and feels like a smooth, tough rope.

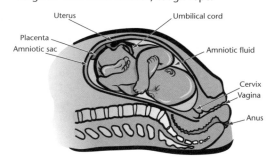

urethra

The tube between the bladder and the opening to the outside of the body. Urine passes through this tube.

urine

The fluid containing water and waste products that is produced by the kidneys, stored in the bladder, and discharged through the urethra when you go to the bathroom.

uterus

A hollow, muscular, pear-shaped organ located in the woman's pelvis. It holds the growing fetus.

vagina

The canal going from the cervix to the outside of the body through which the baby passes during a vaginal birth.

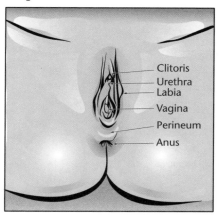

varicose veins

Blood vessels that are swollen, distended, and twisted, showing just beneath the skin, especially on the legs. They result from a slowing of the flow of blood, probably in combination with defects in the valves within the veins and weakened walls of the veins. Pregnancy is often a cause of these. They may disappear at the end of pregnancy.

VDRL test

A blood test to identify women with untreated syphilis.

vernix

A white creamy substance that covers the baby's skin for protection while in the uterus.

voiding

Urinating or peeing.

vulva

The external parts of a woman's reproductive system that surround the opening of the vagina.

Index